U. S. ARMY CHEMICAL CORPS HISTORICAL STUDIES
GAS WARFARE IN WORLD WAR I

GAS WARFARE AT BELLEAU WOOD
June 1918

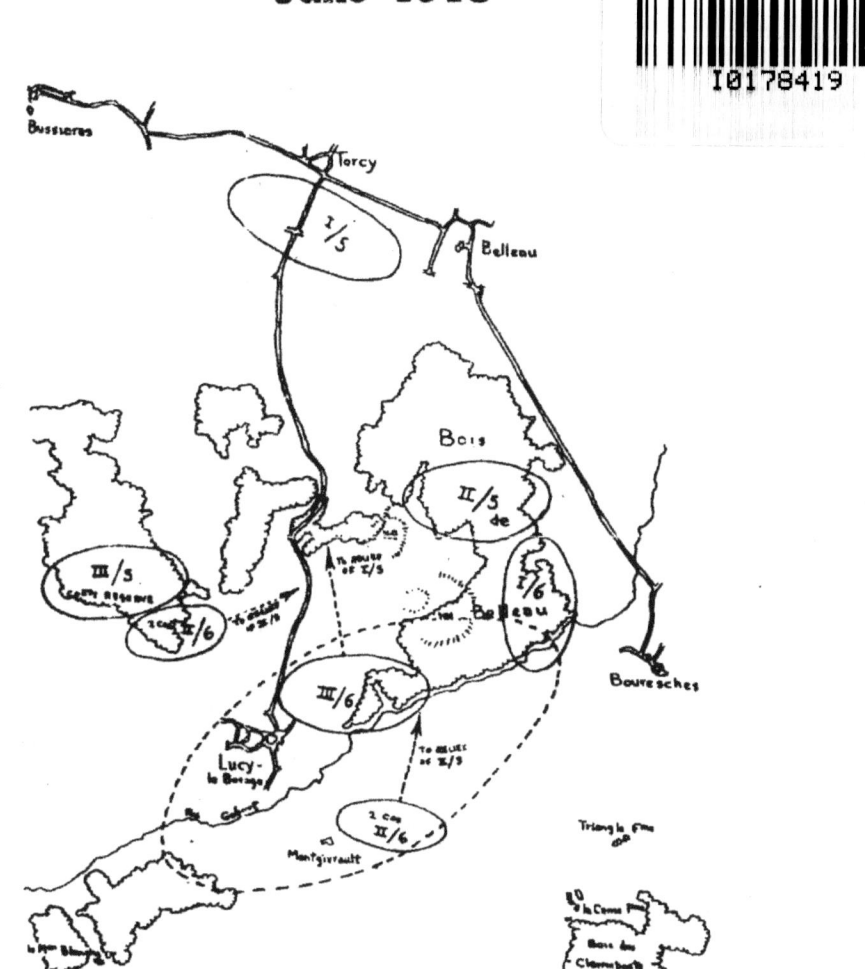

U. S. Army Chemical Corps Historical Office

Office of the Chief Chemical Officer

Washington, D.C.

June 1957

Published by Books Express Publishing
Copyright © Books Express, 2011
ISBN 978-1-78039-564-7

Books Express publications are available from all good retail and online booksellers. For publishing proposals and direct ordering please contact us at: info@books-express.com

Gas Warfare at Belleau Wood
June 1918

by

Rexmond C. Cochrane

GAS WARFARE IN WORLD WAR I

Study Number 1

U.S. ARMY CHEMICAL CORPS
HISTORICAL STUDIES

U.S. Army Chemical Corps Historical Office
Office of the Chief Chemical Officer
Army Chemical Center, Maryland

1957

Gas Warfare at Belleau Wood
June 1918

Prepared by

Rexmond C. Cochrane, Ph.D.

Under contract DA-18-108-CML-6214

with

U.S. Army Chemical Corps

This is an accepted draft study on gas warfare in World War I

W. R. CURRIE
Brigadier General, USA
Asst CCmlO for Planning & Doctrine

Foreword

This is a tentative study of the gas experience of the 2nd Division at Belleau Wood during World War I. This study is not presented as a definitive and official history, but is reproduced for current reference use within the Military Establishment pending the publication of an approved history.

The author was assisted in his research by Mr. David E. Harvey.

Note to Reader: Comments and suggestions relative to accuracy and adequacy of treatment are invited, and may be transmitted to the Chief, U.S. Army Chemical Corps Historical Office, Army Chemical Center, Maryland.

GAS WARFARE AT BELLEAU WOOD
JUNE 1918

Narrative

Background.	1
The Second Division Assembles in France	4
Training in Gas Defense	5
Training in Trench Warfare	8
The Three German Drives, Spring 1918	15
West of Chateau Thierry	17
The Gas Attack of 13-14 June	30
Reprisal and Stalemate	38
Attrition in the German Forces	46
The Gas Attack of June 23-24 and the Capture of Belleau Wood	50
The Taking of Vaux	55

Analysis

German Artillery Fire	63
The Casualties of the 2nd Division	65
Gas Shell Fired by 2nd Division Artillery	69
The Use of Gas at Belleau Wood	71
The Gas Discipline of the 2nd Division	73
The Strategy at Chateau Thierry	76

Maps

Map No. 1. The Battle Ground of World War I	2a
Map No. 2. Situation Map, 2nd Division, Evening of 1 June	17a

Maps

Map No. 3.	Situation & Disposition of 2nd Division, 4-5 June. . . .	20a
Map No. 4.	Situation Map, 4th Reserve Corps (Conta), Noon, 4 June. .	21a
Map No. 5.	Gas Attack on 4th Brigade, 14 June.	32a
Map No. 6.	Situation Map, Corps Conta, Noon, 19 June	46a
Map No. 7.	5th Marine Organization of Belleau Wood	55a
Map No. 8.	Situation Map, Corps Schoeler, 4 July	60a

GAS WARFARE AT BELLEAU WOOD
JUNE 1918

Perhaps the most publicized single unit operation in World War I was the stand of the 2nd Division across the Paris Road and the subsequent battle of that division for Belleau Wood. The artillery, machine gun, and rifle duel fought over the kilometer of terrain near Chateau Thierry in June 1918 has been well described in both Marine and Army publications and in popular and official histories. Many of these accounts acknowledge briefly and in passing the use of gas in the battle. Some fail to mention gas entirely, despite the fact that in this operation, its first independent combat action, the 2nd Division was under some kind of gas attack on 31 of the 35 days of the campaign.

Neither in manuscript or published histories of the 2nd Division nor in Marine accounts of the action in Belleau Wood that have been consulted for this report is the gas story given more than incidental treatment. Yet for a period of three or four days following the gas attack of 14-15 June, a determined effort by the German forces opposite might well have shattered the entire front of the 2nd Division and opened the way to Meaux and Paris.

Background

On August 4, 1914, seven German Armies totaling almost 1,700,000 troops launched their great wheeling attack through Belgium, Luxembourg, and France, intending the quick conquest of France envisioned by the von Schlieffen Plan of 1906-07. The Armies, using multiples of machine guns and heavy artillery in new tactical employments, penetrated to within twenty miles of Paris and an equal distance south of the Marne to the east of Paris before they could be brought to a stop on September 9th.

At that point, a series of mistakes that had been made by von Moltke, the German Chief of Staff, and his Army commanders, in conjunction with tactics of Joffre, forced the withdrawal of the German Armies back to the Aisne. With this check, both German and Allied Armies attempted repeated flanking maneuvers, which resulted in extending their forces in a long slow S curve aslant northern France, reaching from Nieuport on the Belgian coast down to Belfort, near the border of Switzerland. By the end of 1914, the entire line was committed to trench warfare, and was to remain fixed until early 1917 "without varying so much as ten miles in either direction" (see Map No. 1).[1]

Although great battles were fought along the line throughout 1917, the single principal change occurred in March, when the German forces in the devastated Noyon salient made a planned withdrawal to the recently completed Hindenburg line, thereby shortening their front NE of Paris by twenty miles. More important were the battle innovations introduced in 1917.

At the battle of Arras, north of the Noyon salient, in April, the British first used their new gas weapon, the Livens projector. In producing a gas cloud at a distance from the point of discharge, the Livens maintained the high concentration of gas obtained with cylinder projection, yet

---

[1] G. L. McEntee, Military History of the World War (New York: Scribner, 1937), p. 83; B. H. Liddell Hart, The Real War, 1914-1918 (Boston: Little, Brown) 1931, Ch. III.

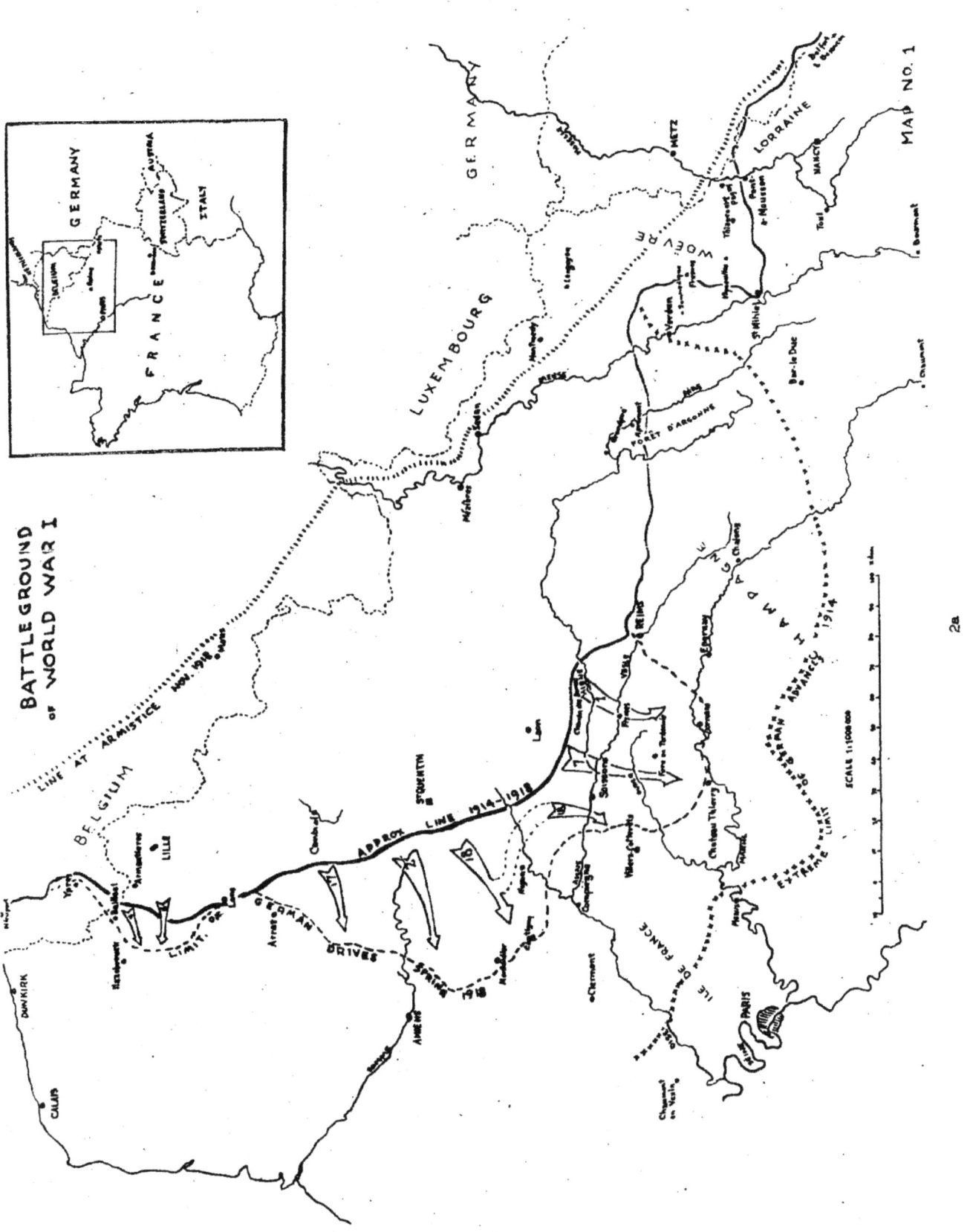

achieved the surprise effect of gas shell fire.[2] The Germans had a similar projector by December. The 4-inch Stokes mortar was next developed, for rapid fire of gas, phosphorus, and thermite, particularly to neutralize machine gun nests. At Arras, also, sixty British tanks took part in battle for the first time, but not until at Cambrai, in November, when 324 tanks were deployed, were effective tactics formulated for their use.

In the summer of 1917, the Germans first used their improved green cross shell (diphosgene), firing over 100,000 rounds in a single bombardment at Verdun.[3] The French M2 mask was developed for protection against the green cross gases. At Nieuport and at the third battle of Ypres, in July and August of that year, the new German mustard gas, in yellow cross shell, was used for the first time. The French did not get their yperite (mustard gas) to the battlefield until June 1918, and the British did not use it until September 1918. Also in the summer of 1917, the Germans introduced blue cross shell (diphenylchlorarsine with some HE), in an attempt

---

[2] The British persisted with cloud gas attacks because prevailing winds on the Western front favored the Allies, and the British knew its deadly effect. The Germans, who had used cloud gas principally for casualty effects and not in the attack, gave it up because of the enormous effort required to mount a cloud attack.

[3] Although the first gas attack, with chlorine projected from cylinders, occurred in April 1915, as early as October 1914, the Germans constructed their first gas shell, to discharge an irritant substance and pulverize it upon explosion to form a cloud of dust. The first effective German gas projectile for the heavy field howitzer, containing a lachrymatory agent, was fired in January 1915; and the first lethal gas shell (phosgene, in the green cross shell) was used by the Germans in December 1915. The French phosgene shell appeared in the field in March 1916, and was countered soon after by the German introduction of chlorpicrin shell, to induce nausea and removal of the mask and thereby ensure effectiveness of the lethal gas.

to penetrate the British respirator.[4]

1917 also saw for the first time planes machine-gunning ground troops and bombing troop concentrations from the air. An American suggestion in January 1918 concerning "the use of aeroplanes for discharging gas upon the enemy" was promptly dismissed. "For reasons of policy, it is considered extremely unwise to make any reference whatever to this subject."[5]

The Second Division Assembles in France

The United States entered the war against Germany on 6 April 1917, and two months later the initial elements of the 1st Division, organized on 24 May 1917, sailed for France. The components of the 2nd Division, not formally organized as such until 22 September 1917, arrived in France between July 1917 and February 1918, when the concentration of the Division, less its artillery, was completed and its systematic training begun at Bourmont, in the Haute Marne. As they embarked for France, the commander of the 5th MG Battalion later said, "Not one man in ten knew a machine gun from a cream separator and many had yet to learn the first fundamentals of military life." Until organized training began in January, the marines and infantrymen who were to make up the division "were scattered all over France and England," doing stevedore work, building roads, barracks, and warehouses, loading and unloading freight cars, and cutting firewood.

---

[4] See Maj Gen C. H. Foulkes, Gas! (Edinburgh & London, 1934), pp. 304 ff.

[5] Ltr, CCO to Comdt Army Gas School, 4 Feb 18, sub: Lecture by Lt Anderson Gas as an Offensive Weapon (GHQ AEF box 1726 fol. S). Cf. earlier ltr, C Gas Serv AEF to CofS AEF, 7 Sep 17, sub: Memo on the Tactical Use of Gas in Warfare, which suggested that "gas by plane, however, may be attempted in the future" (GHQ AEF Box 1727, fol. P-10).

As assembled, the principal components of Maj. Gen. Omar Bundy's 2nd Division were the 3rd Infantry Brigade, Brig. Gen. Edward M. Lewis, commanding, made up of the 9th Infantry, 23rd Infantry, and 5th Machine Gun Battalion; the 4th Marine Brigade, Brig. Gen. James G. Harbord, commanding, composed of the 5th and 6th Marines and 6th Machine Gun Battalion (Marine); and divisional troops, including the 4th Machine Gun Battalion, 2nd Engineers, 1st Field Signal Battalion, and Headquarters Troops. Headquarters, Military Police, and Supply, Engineer, and Sanitary trains completed the divisional forces assembled in France.

The other major component of the Division, the 2nd Field Artillery Brigade, Brig. Gen. William Chamberlaine (after 27 June, Col. A. J. Bowley), commanding, made up of the 12th, 15th, and 17th Field Artillery, and the 2nd Trench Mortar Battalion, was assembled and began its training at the French artillery center at Le Valdahon, near Besancon and the Swiss border, on 30 January 1918. On 21 March it joined the division near Verdun.

Training in Gas Defense

A report summarizing the gas training of the 2nd Division at Bourmont between 15 December 1917 and 15 March 1918 said that in this period

> all received one hour per day gas training and in addition men wore the masks during drills. Surprise alarms were given frequently. All men were passed through lachrimatory and chlorine gas in gas chamber. All men were equipped with both the French M2 mask and British S.B.R. [small box respirator]. It was believed that many of the gas casualties later were caused by men changing to the M2 mask. The drills and lectures were conducted by the gas personnel or the Units under the supervision of the Division Gas Officer. All men at the time of putting through the gas chamber were given a lecture by the Division Gas Officer. During all periods out of lines gas defense instruction was carried on whenever possible, including respirator drills, gas chamber, lectures and use of lachrimatory grenades. While the Division was in lines respirators were inspected

frequently and units not in front line continued mask drills.[6]

While some information on gas warfare seems to have reached elements of the 2nd Division receiving preliminary training in the States, there appears to have been no gas defense instruction at the troop level.[7] The gas training program in France began with the formation of the Gas Service, AEF, on 3 September 1917 and the preparation on 1 October of Pamphlet No. 253, Defensive Measures against Gas Attacks.[8] Its fifteen pages of "Standing Orders" described the detection of shell and cloud gases, giving special attention to the hazards of mustard gas; inspection of anti-gas supplies; procedure for gas mask drill; the warning system for cloud and shell attacks; gasproofing of dugouts; and behavior during and after a gas attack. It emphasized that within 12 miles of the front line a box respirator or mask was always to be carried, that within 5 miles a box respirator must be carried, and within 2 miles the box respirator and mask must be carried, with the respirator in the "alert" position. Following a gas attack, the respirator was to be removed only by permission of an officer. (This was later specified as an American officer, for French officers and NCOs were believed to order removal of masks too soon.)

---

[6] Ltr, DGO 2nd Div to C CWS, 8 Feb 19, sub: Circular Ltr No. 89 (WD Hist Box 300, 33.6); also in GAF-2S (2nd Div Summaries). GAF records are at the Army Chemical Center, Md.

[7] Tng Memos No. 1 and 2 (13, 23 Apr 1917), Hq Southern Dept, Fort Sam Houston, Texas (GHQ AEF Box 1513, fol. 2).

[8] GHQ AEF Box 1727, fol. D. A 75-page revision was issued by GHQ AEF the following month for issue "Down to include all officers and organizations, all combat units."

With the establishment in November 1917 of the AEF gas school at Langres and the 1st Army Corps gas school at Gondrescourt, the general principles of gas training set down in the AEF Pamphlet were followed in the initial six-day courses of instruction, consisting of a 45-minute lecture and 1½ hours of practical application each day. The instruction in the 40-page Manual, Program of Training in Gas Defense for Divisional Anti-Gas Schools, prepared by the Army War College, 23 October 1917, paralleled that in Pamphlet No. 253, except that there was no mention of mustard gas in the manual.[9] This was remedied in the comprehensive manual issued by the Army War College in December and January, entitled, Gas Warfare, comprising Part I: German Methods of Offense, Part II: Methods of Defense Against Gas Attacks, Part III: Methods of Training in Defensive Measures, and Part IV: The Offensive in Gas Warfare.[10]

The Second Division did not receive either its M2 masks or its respirators until late in December 1917, and Regimental Gas Officers and Company Gas NCOs were not appointed until early in January. As a consequence, inspection reports in January indicated that the gas readiness of the Division was extremely sketchy in every respect.[11] A Revised Program of Training for the 2nd Division was set up to provide for two weeks of troop training in gas defense in February, while special GHQ AEF gas training programs of 10, 18, and 20 hours' duration were issued for the engineer and sanitary

---

[9] 2nd Div Box 225, Hq Misc Data; WD Hist Box 205, 54.3, GHQ AEF Boxes 1725, 1726.

[10] Parts II and III only are in WD Hist Box 205.

[11] Ltr, GO 2nd Div to CinC AEF, 22 Dec 17, sub: Rpt on Anti-Gas Tng in 2nd Div (2nd Div Box 106); memo for C Tng Sec, 9 Jan 18, sub: Visit to 2nd Div; memo C Tng Sec for CofS, 30 Jan 18, sub: Tactical Inspection and Future Tng of 2nd Div (2nd Div Box 33).

troops and medical officers.[12]

Training in Trench Warfare

On 13 March 1918, the 2nd Division, less its artillery, moved to the quiet sector of the French Second Army front near Sommedieue, SE of Verdun, where it joined the French X Corps in the line just NW of St. Mihiel, for training in the tactics of trench warfare. There, with its artillery in support a week later, it was trained by battalion, regiment, and brigade, and participated with the divisions of the French X Corps and later the French II Colonial Corps of the French Second Army in the occupation of the Toulon and Troyons Sectors of the front line in Lorraine.[13]

With the arrival of the American forces in the area, the sector ceased to be quiet. Under the provocation of raiding patrols, enemy artillery fire increased daily, and on 21 March, the 2nd Division experienced gas for the first time, when over a 12-hour period 25 unidentified 77mm gas shells were fired into the Bois Bonchamp, but "Without any serious inconvenience to our troops."[14] Four gas shells fell in the sector the next morning and four more on the 27th, causing the first gas casualty reported by the 2nd Division.[15] On 31 March, incidental to a German raid on the French lines, heavy artillery

---

[12] 2nd Div Boxes 32 and 33, 50.4, Box 63, 50.7.

[13] Hist Sec, AWC, *Order of Battle...AEF* (Washington: GPO, 1931), pp. 22-29.

[14] Summary of Intelligence, 20-21 Mar 18. These SOI, unnumbered until 12 Apr, are in the National Archives bound series, *Records of the Second Division, Ft. Sam Houston and Army War College, 1924-28*, Vol. 9. Hereafter referred to as *Records*.

[15] War Diary, 28 Mar (*Records* 6).

fire fell on the 2nd Division area, including 65 77mm gas shells, apparently "in response to the activity of our own artillery." Again the gas was "without any damaging effect." The only casualties reported were six men wounded by the shell fire.[16]

The first extensive use of gas on 2nd Division troops occurred on 6 April when, in searching out the divisional batteries, 750 105mm gas shells fell around four of the battery positions and over 1,000 HE shells on five other gun sites. Division headquarters recorded no gas casualties and only three men of the 23rd Infantry wounded by the shell fire.[17] But the 2nd F.A. Brigade, reporting later on its operations near Verdun, observed that although "casualties were slight, nearly all of them were due to gas bombardments of the battery positions."[18]

Mixtures of gas shell with heavy HE fire continued daily on the batteries and troop areas from 9 to 12 April, with no gas casualties reported in divisional records. However, a Report on Gas Attack from the 9th Infantry on 10 April said that 125 diphosgene shells had surprised a battalion at Violette the previous afternoon, causing 12 severe casualties. The next morning approximately 150 yperite shells fell on the edge of Rouvrois, but

---

[16]
 SOI, 31 Mar-1 Apr; War Diary, 1 Apr. Spencer, History of Gas Attacks upon AEF during the World War (EACD 460, 15 Feb 1928), l.93, reports 8 men slightly gassed by palite on this date.

[17]
 SOI, 6-7 Apr; War Diary, 8 Apr.

[18]
 Rpt, Opns of 2nd FA Brig, 30 May-25 Jun (Records 9).

the wind carried the vapor away from the 9th Infantry troops near there.[19]

Then, following a shelling with approximately 400 HE rounds on the previous evening, between 4:00 and 8:00 a.m. on 13 April, "the first gas bombardment of any size...probably in retaliation for our artillery activity during the afternoon" struck the 1st Battalion, 6th Marines, in reserve in the Bonchamp sector. Of approximately 3,000-3,600 shells, the division reported 1,800 were gas, the greater part yellow cross, the remainder blue cross.[20] One mustard-filled 105mm struck a shack where 60 men were sleeping. Gas casualties were first reported as 2 officers and 108 men, later corrected to 6 officers and 271 men, most of them "only slightly gassed." No HE casualties were reported. The troops evacuated the area and chlorinate of lime was spread to decontaminate it.[21]

Other reports were more explicit. "The number of casualties was inexcusably large, 277 being evacuated up until noon of April 14th," said the Corps Gas Officer. "Of these all suffered from conjuctivitis, many having infected lungs and several are badly blistered, especially between the legs ....practically all...caused by the ignorance of the officers concerning the persistence of this gas, and the consequent premature removal of masks (half an hour after the bombardment) and the failure to promptly evacuate the camp." He added that the Regimental Gas Officer arrived on the scene at 9:00 the following morning, and no notice was given to the Division or Corps

---

[19] GAF-2A (fol. 2nd Div Attacks).

[20] Hanslian, Gasangriffe an der Amerikanischen Front, no date, p. 94 (CMLHO), says 4540 blue cross, 1430 green cross, and 5270 yellow cross were used, in weather unsuited for gas bombardment.

[21] SOI 26, 12-13 Apr; War Diary, 13 Apr.

Gas Officers until the afternoon of the 14th.[22] A history of the Marine brigade was to say: "All officers and 220 men of the 74th Co., 6th Marines, were evacuated in a serious condition, over 40 men dying later as a result of this first bombardment."[23]

A letter on 19 April said: "Capt. Goss has advised court martial for the Company Officers, 74th Co....Major Montgomery, the Division Inspector, has been inspecting the Division on this recommendation and is trying very hard to fix the blame on the Gas Service. Capt. Goss informed him that the line officers, so far, had taken gas and gas officers as a joke, and now that gas casualties had occurred, were demanding an explanation of the gas officers attached to the unit."[24]

A strong German raid with five companies (over 400 men) against the Rouvrois sector occupied by the 9th Infantry at 11:00 p.m. that same night, 13 April, apparently to gain information about American forces in the area, was preceded by a six-hour barrage with 700 HE and 4,500 mixed gas and HE shells -- "the heaviest yet experienced by American troops in this sector." The gas included "lachrymatose," followed by phosgene, then mustard. Casualties were estimated at one officer and 4 men killed by the HE and 2

---

[22] Rpt of Gas Attack on 6th Marines, Capt B.C. Goss, CGO 1st AC, 14 Apr (GAF 2-A, 2nd Div Attacks). A supplement to this rpt on 17 Apr said total casualties were 295, with 9 deaths. Hanslian, p. 95, has 295 Marine casualties, 5 in 23rd Inf, and 53 in 9th Inf.

[23] MS, Brig Gen Wendell C. Neville, Hist of 4th Brig, Marine Corps, AEF, Oct 23, 1917-Dec 31, 1918, p. 4 (2nd Div Box 44). See also Hist of 6th Regt, in 2nd Div Box 68,11.4, Spencer, I. 101-106, records 295 casualties, 29 deaths.

[24] Ltr, CGO 1st C [1st Lt Earl C. Popp, SC for Capt B. C. Goss, Eng] to C Gas Serv AEF, 19 Apr, Sub: Report (GAF, 1st Corps Misc).

officers and 50 men gassed. The 9th Infantry Gas Officer reported 2,000 77mm and 105mm green and yellow cross shells, causing 53 casualties, 22 of them due to mustard. Owing to the situation, he said, the men could not move from their positions. Some of the men were gassed changing from the S.B.R. to the M2 mask when the irritancy of the first gas made wearing the S.B.R. difficult.[25] By 5:00 a.m. the counterattacking 9th Infantry had driven off the raiders, who left 11 prisoners and 61 dead, at a cost to the regiment of 7 killed, 42 wounded, and 19 missing.[26]

On 4 April, ten days before this gas attack, the 2nd Division had issued Memorandum No. 34 repeating the gas defense instructions of Pamphlet 253 on the dangers of mustard persistency and premature removal of the mask. Yet Memorandum 37, 17 April, reported that in the recent gas attack practically all casualties had been caused by ignorance of the officers concerning the persistency of mustard, premature removal of masks, and failure to evacuate the camp promptly.[27]

Daily patrols, sniping, and light gas shelling continued in this quiet sector, while artillery activity ranged from normal to subnormal in the weeks that followed, as sizeable numbers of the German forces opposite the 2nd

---

[25] AEF Pamphlet 253 had contained instructions on changing from the S.B.R. to the M2. On 5 June, however, all French masks were ordered turned in to DGOs, to prevent troops from changing masks during an attack (memo for Regtl and Sep Orgn Comds, 2nd Div Box 106; Weekly Sum of Info, Gas Serv Intel Sec, 5 June, in WD Hist Box 289.

[26] SOI 27, 13-14 Apr; supp to War Diary, 14 Apr; corr in SOI 31, 19-20 Apr; Rpt on Gas Attack, 15 Apr (GAF-2A).

[27] 2nd Div Box 36, 64.4.

- 12 -

Division lines were pulled out and sent north to the fighting along the Somme, and battle-weary enemy troops from the Somme took their place.[28] Results of the desultory gas shelling were erratic. Thirty 105mm green and yellow cross shells, for example, fell in ten minutes on 21 April, causing 15 casualties in the 15th F.A. On the other hand, "a short severe gas bombardment" of 100 77mm mustard shells put down on a company of the 23rd Infantry in the line near La Croix between 2:30-3:00 a.m. on 7 May reportedly caused no casualties.[29]

On 9 May, the 2nd Division began its withdrawal from the Toulon front for refitting near Bar-le-Duc, and on 18 May entrained for Chaumont-en-Vexin, NW of Paris, in the rear of the Fifth French Army, where it was to undergo a period of training in the tactics of open warfare, preparatory to relieving 1st Division forces in the Montdidier sector.

During the two months in training in the Toulon-Troyon sector, the 2nd Division Surgeon reported treating 347 gas cases, 161 wounded, 91 injured, 934 sick, and 3 PNs.[30] A somewhat different record of casualties, compiled by the 2nd Division Statistical Section for the period 15 Mar-30 May, (Records 6) shows total casualties of 12 officers and 826 men, of which 4 officers and 319 men were evacuated as gas cases.

---

[28] Supp to War Diary, 28 Apr.

[29] Jnl of Opns, 7 May (Records 6); Rpt on Gas Attack, 7 May, (GAF-2A).

[30] Ltr, Div Surg to CG G-3 2nd Div, 22 Feb 19, sub: Rpt of Opns, Med Dept, 2nd Div, Mar 16 to May 15, 1918; supp to War Diary, 15 May.

Of interest is a 1st Army Corps report for that period on the effectiveness of gas against the American Army. After recording total field casualties in the Corps of 4,190, with gas casualties of 2,262, up to 15 May 1918, the report said:

> The importance of a vigorous gas program is shown by the increasing number of gas casualties suffered by the First Army Corps. The figures are unofficial and incomplete but are unquestionably too low, as reports of gas casualties have only recently been regularly made. Even as it is, gas casualties are 54% of all casualties....due to inexperience in gas warfare and a great lack of appreciation of the seriousness of gas (GAF, fol. 1st C).

Alarmed by the inadequacies of individual and company gas discipline revealed in the first major gas attack on the division, the command instituted gas training programs as soon as the troops came out of the line.[31] While refitting at Bar-le-Duc, the entire division was retrained by its Regimental Gas Officers in gas mask and gas defense drill every evening of its stay there.[32] Further training at Chaumont-en-Vexin was conducted as a result of General Order 33, 1 May, which described again the necessary conduct of troops in the "alert" zones and spelled out the duties of gas officers and gas NCOs.[33] Another order, first issued in early April again required all officers and men to practice wearing the respirator one hour a day while performing regular duties.[34] Special attention was given to the peculiar hazards of mustard gas, described in Pamphlet 253, emphasized in

---

[31] See Memo No. 48, 2nd Eng, 29 Apr (2nd Div Box 85, 10.2).

[32] 2nd Div Box 33, 50.4.

[33] This order was revised as GO 39, 28 May, without any essential changes. Both in (Records 9).

[34] See Memos 113, 119, 23rd Inf, 13, 19 Apr (2nd Div Box 63, 64.4, AG Memos).

- 14 -

General Order 33, and in the Weekly Summaries of Information of the Gas Service Intelligence Section.[35]

There is reason to believe that one cause of the poor discipline when troops were confronted by mustard gas shell was the amount of training time expended on methods of defense against cloud attack. All during the spring of 1918, Intelligence reported that cloud attacks were imminent, and training had been oriented accordingly.[36] Actually, of the 320 or more gas attacks made by the Germans on the AEF, not one was a cylinder cloud attack and only six were projector attacks.

The Three German Drives, Spring 1918

As the 2nd Division had entrained for the Toulon sector in the Spring of 1918, the German High Command put in operation its plans for "the greatest military task ever imposed upon an army."[37] A series of large-scale assaults were to be mounted against the Allied lines, which, Ludendorff was convinced, in view of the tired French and British forces and the depleted reserves backing them up, would break under the onslaught. The success of these attacks ranks with that of the advance to "the Marne in 1914 as the two gravest military crises of the World War."[38]

---

[35] See WSIs for 27 Mar, 4 Apr, 10 Apr in WD Hist Box 289 and others in 2nd Div Box 106.

[36] See GO 33 and WDIs, above.

[37] McEntee, p. 467.

[38] Hart, p. 387.

A total of 74 German divisions in three Armies (the 17th, 2nd and 18th) made the initial assault on 21 March against the four British Armies holding the line from the Oise north to the Channel, with the intention of severing British contact with the French forces to the south and pushing the British to the sea. By 4 April, a forty-mile bulge had been made in the British lines and the Germans had achieved mobility and maneuverability again after three years of static warfare. Then, outrunning their supplies, the German Armies lost their forward impetus and the first great attack came to a halt before Amiens. On 9 April, two more German Armies (the 4th and 6th), astride the French-Belgian border, launched a second assault against the British and Portugese forces south of Ypres (see Map No. 1). After a ten-mile advance, this drive too stopped short of success.

Before continuing the attack in the north, to drive the British into the sea, Ludendorff set in motion his third great attack, on 27 May, against the French armies on the Soissons-Reims front where they joined the British. For this assault, three German Armies (a portion of the 18th, the 7th and 1st) numbering 42 divisions, with 3,719 guns, secretly assembled along the Chemin des Dames. The assault was apparently intended as a diversion, while German forces to the north regrouped and communications were improved, to draw back those French forces that had gone to the assistance of the British and to draw French reserves to the Aisne.[39] The success of this diversion almost resulted in an Allied disaster.

Facing the 18th, 7th, and 1st German Armies, but unaware either of the numbers of enemy troops or their readiness for attack, were the 10th, 6th,

---
[39] McEntee, p. 485.

- 16 -

and 5th French Armies. Preceded by tanks, nineteen divisions of the German 7th and 1st Armies, spanning a 25-mile front, jumped off on the attack at 4:30 a.m. on 27 May. Eight French and three British divisions along the Chemin des Dames front, all resting in this quiet sector at the time, were met by the surprise offense and fell back. By noon the Germans were crossing the Aisne, by evening they were across the Vesle. On the third day they were at the Marne, 60 miles from Paris, spread across a 40-kilometer front running approximately from Soissons to Chateau Thierry, and 65,000 prisoners and great stores of abandoned supplies were in their hands.[40]

That same day, 30 May, the 2nd and 3rd Divisions, then in training at Chaumont-en-Vexin and near Chaumont, respectively, were put at the disposal of the French and assigned to the 6th French Army. Rushed by truck to the front, the combat elements of the 2nd Division were sent to the XXI French Corps as reinforcement, to stop the German advance along the Chateau Thierry-Paris road.[41]

West of Chateau Thierry

The combat units of the Division detrucked and assembled in the area NE of Meaux. Shortly after midnight, 1 June, a French order was received to send the 9th Infantry and 6th Marines by forced march to Montreuil-aux-Lions, to take up positions north and south of the Chateau Thierry-Paris

---

[40] Hart, pp. 373, 411 ff.

[41] McEntee, p. 487; Field Order 6, 2nd Div, 1 Jun (Records 1); Jnl O, 30 May (Records 6).

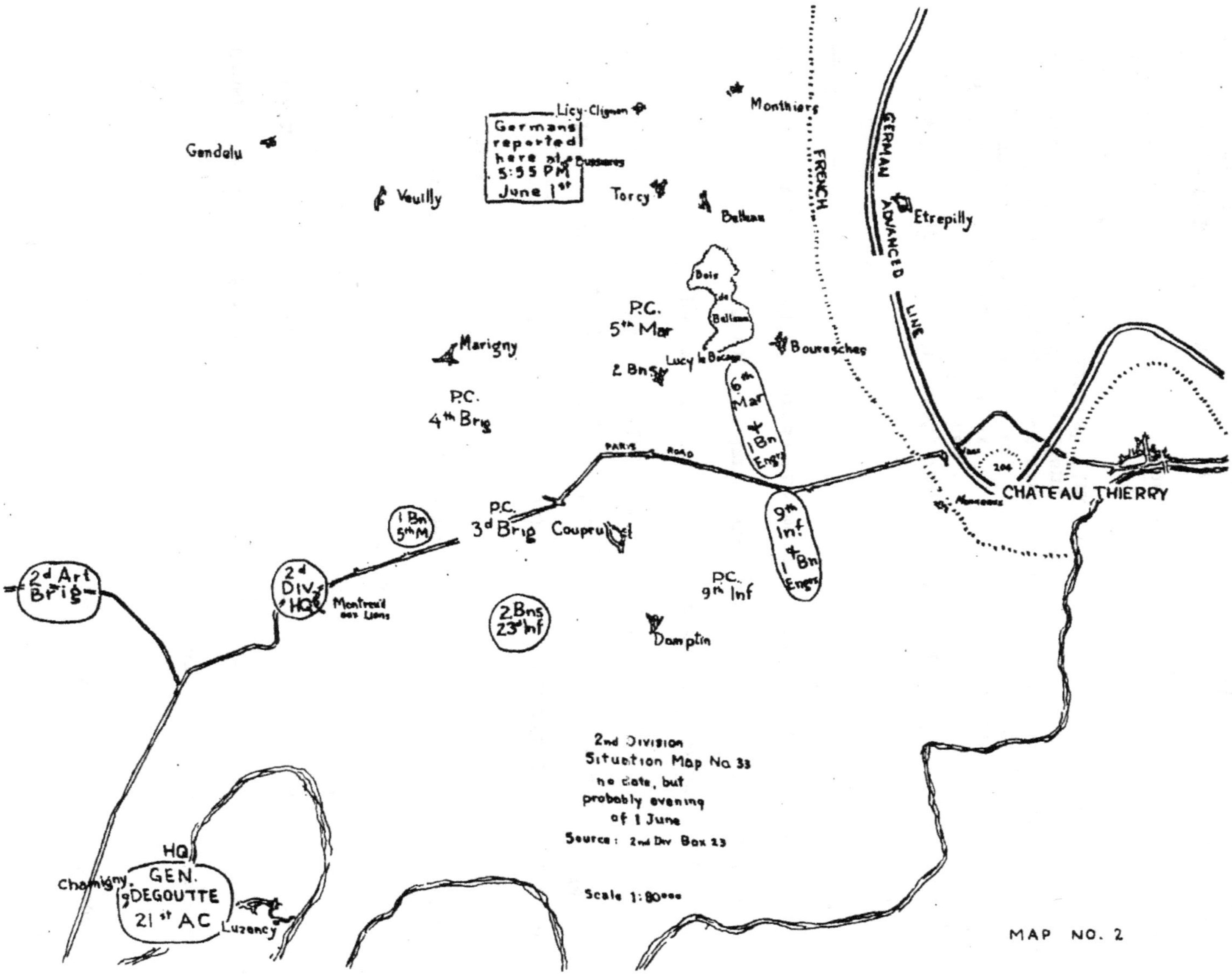
Gendalu
Vaully
Germans reported here at 5:55 PM June 1st
Licy-Clignon
Bussiares
Torcy
Monthiers
Belleau
FRENCH
GERMAN ADVANCED LINE
Etrepilly
Bois de Belleau
P.C. 5th Mar
2 Bns
Lucy le Bocage
Bouresches
Marigny
P.C. 4th Brig
6th Mar + 1 Bn Engrs
PARIS ROAD
204
CHATEAU THIERRY
P.C. 3d Brig
Coupru
1 Bn 5th M
9th Inf + 1 Bn Engrs
P.C. 9th Inf
2d Art Brig
2d DIV HQ
Montreuil aux Lions
2 Bns 23d Inf
Domptin
2nd Division Situation Map No. 33
no date, but probably evening of 1 June
Source: 2nd Div Box 23
Scale 1:80000
HQ GEN. DEGOUTTE 21st AC
Chamigny
Luzancy

MAP NO. 2

road, where the Germans were expected momentarily. Following a second message that morning, the 23rd Infantry under Col. Paul B. Malone, with a battalion of the 5th Marines and the 5th Machine Gun Battalion -- a total of 5,000 men -- was rushed to fill a gap in the lines of the 43rd French Division at Gandelu (see Map No. 2).[42]

When Maj. Gen. Omar Bundy, commander of the 2nd Division, reported to General Degoutte of the XXI Corps at his headquarters at Chamigny on 1 June,[43] the 6th French Army units in the line of battle west of Chateau Thierry comprised from left to right, the VII Corps, two depleted divisions (the 43rd and 164th) of the XXI Corps, and a single division of the XXXVIII Corps. The 43rd French Division was fighting to the north of the Paris road, the 164th French Division on the south of that road.

The 7th German Army units opposite the French XXI Corps had been identified as the 197th, 237th and 10th Divisions of Corps Conta.[44] To the right were the two other divisions of Corps Conta, the 231st and 36th. That day, 1 June, the Corps was reported on the general line St. Gengoulph-Etrepilly-Chateau Thierry, its immediate objective Licy Clignon-Monthiers-Hill 204 and a bridgehead across the Marne below Chateau Thierry.[45]

---

[42] Jnl O, 1 Jun.

[43] McEntee, p. 487. MS hist, The Second Division at Chateau Thierry, by Hist Sec GS AEF, 1918, p. 12, has a pencilled note by Col Preston Brown, CofS, 2nd Div, for May 31-Jun 1: "Bundy in Paris-PB" (2nd Div Box 8, 18.2). This is confirmed by Lt Col Hayes, Div Regulating Officer, who adds that in the conference at Chamigny, "The French Commander's opinion was that a retreat should be made, and he evidently considered everything lost, and the Germans practically the victors" (Interv at Hq 2nd Div, 12 Dec 1918, 2nd Div Box 4, 11.4).

[44] This was the 4th Reserve Corps, named for its commander, von Conta.

[45] Corps Order, Opns No. 499, 1:30 a.m., 1 Jun (doc 69, 231st Inf Div, War Diaries of German Units Opposing the Second Division, AWC, 1930-32, Vol. 4). Hereafter referred to as War Diaries.

- 18 -

The next day, 2 June, the forces of the 2nd Division north of Montreuil-aux-Lions and the remaining elements of the Division coming into the area moved up to cover almost a 9,000-yard front, along the line Bois de Veuilly-Hill 142-Lucy le Bocage-Triangle-Bois des Clerembauts-le Thiolet.[46] At the same time, advancing German machine gun and infantry units took Bussiares, Torcy, and the Bois de Belleau on the evening of 2 June, as the french continued to fall back.[47] At midnight, a message to the 2nd Division from the French Commanding General read: "The American troops will maintain at all costs the line of support they occupy." [48]

On the night of 3-4 June, the slowly retreating French forces began to retire through the line of the 2nd Division. That same night, the batteries of the 12th F.A. came into position in the vicinities of La Voie du Chatel, Ferme Paris, and Coupru, with the 15th F.A. to the E and SE of Domptin, and the 17th F.A., with its 155s, spanning the Paris road.[49]

The 23rd Infantry and supporting units returned to the Division on the night of 4-5 June, and on 5 June, reinforced by seven elements of the 37th, 232nd, 236th, and 333rd French Field Artillery which had remained in position, the 2nd Division alone held the sector, with the 5th and 6th

---

[46] Field Message, CofS to Col Malone, 23rd Inf, 2 Jun (Records 4); FO 7, 2nd Div, 3 p.m., 3 Jun. All FMs in Vol. 4 unless otherwise specified.

[47] FM 21st Fr Army Corps to 2nd Div, 1:35 a.m., 3 Jun; Corps Order, Opns No. 512, 12:30 a.m., 3 Jun (doc 69, 231st Inf Div, War Diaries 4).

[48] FM 2nd Div to 4th Brig, 1 a.m., 3 Jun.

[49] MS Hist of 2nd FA Brig, p. 6 (2nd Div Box 77); Opns of 2nd FA Brig, 30 May-25 Jun (Records 9) says the 156 pieces of 2nd Div artillery on 3 Jun were situated N of Montreuil, near La Loge, and near Domptin.

Marines, the 23rd and 9th Infantry, in that order along the front. The 10th French Colonial Division (replacing the 164th) with units of the American 3rd Division was on the right of the 2nd Division, the 167th French Division (replacing the 43rd) on its left. The 2nd Division front, which for a time had spanned almost 20 kilometers, from the north edges of the Bois de Veuilly to La Nouette, was, with the readjustments in the French lines, shortened to about 9 kilometers, extending from south of Hill 142 to south of Monneaux (Map No. 3).[50]

Meanwhile, patrols on 3-4 June confirmed the presence of the enemy to the north of Hill 142, west of Bois de Belleau, and to the east of the Bois des Clerembauts and Bois de la Marette. Having occupied Bussiares, Torcy, and the Bois de Belleau, the German forces had halted in their pursuit of the French to await reserve supplies and munitions and the advance of their heavy artillery. They had set up points of resistance and had dug in temporary shelters. With the artillery at hand, they probed and harassed the forces before them, but without the ability to exercise any real pressure. On 4 June, the units opposite the 2nd Division were identified as the <u>197th and 237th Infantry</u> and the <u>10th Reserve Divisions</u> of <u>Corps Conta</u>, extending

---

[50] Rpt, Lt Col W. D. Grant GS to Col Fox Conner Asst CofS G-3 Hq AEF, 4 Jun (supp to War Diary, 4 Jun); Jnl O, 5 Jun; FO 8, 2nd Div, 5 Jun; MS hist, The Second Division at Chateau Thierry, pp. 17-19 (2nd Div Box 8).

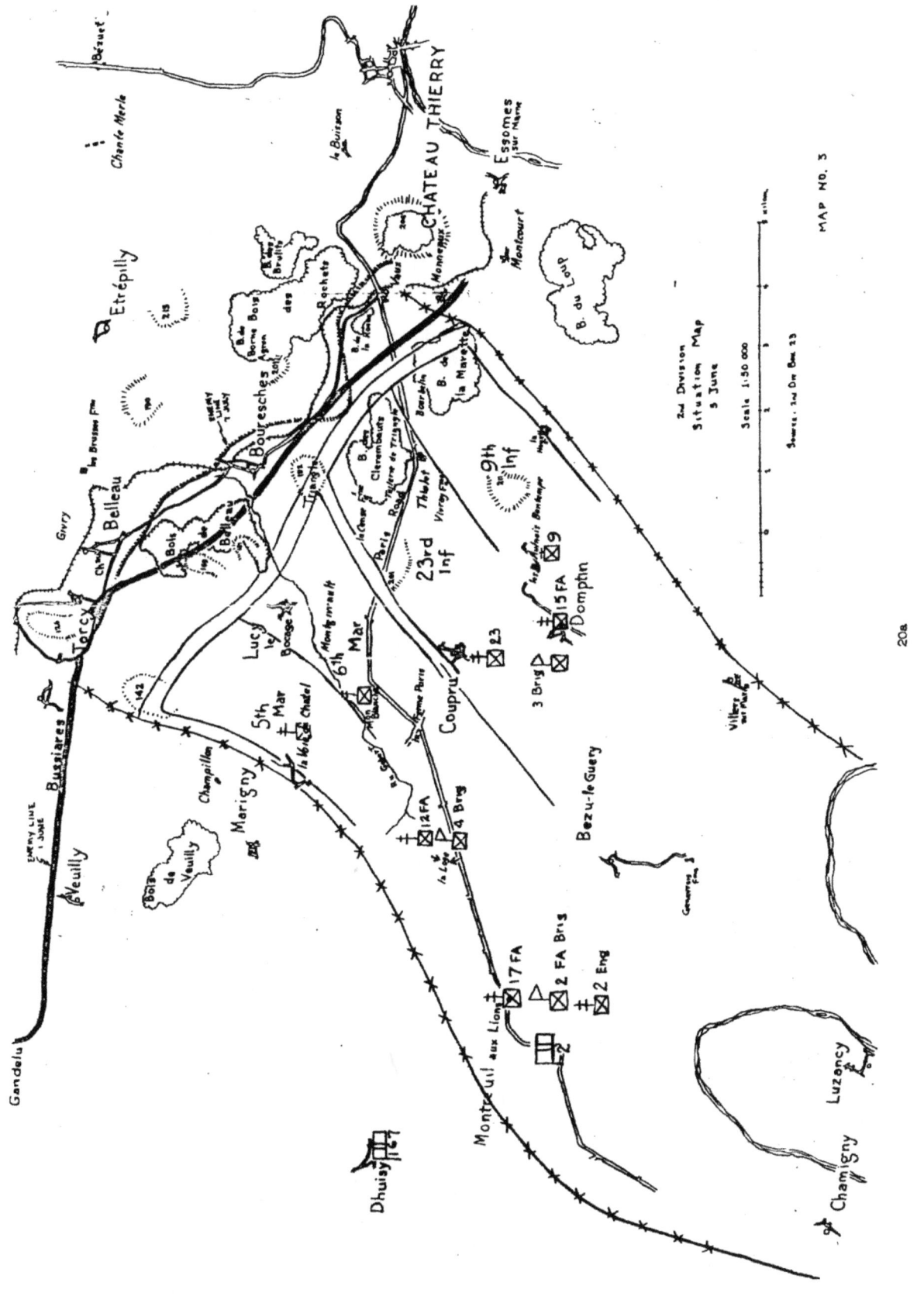

from North of Veuilly to Torcy, Torcy to Bouresches, and Bouresches to Montcourt (Map No. 4).[51]

At midnight, 3-4 June, a Corps Conta order said that in the continuing attack of the 7th Army towards Paris, Corps Conta had been assigned to protect the Army's left flank. To accomplish this, the Corps must advance to "a position that is especially suited for defense." That line of defense would be Veuilly-Marigny-La Voie de Chatel-Hill 201-Le Thoilet-Hill 204. The units making the advance would be the 5th Guard, the 197th, 237th, 28th and 231st Divisions, in line. Reconnaissance and preparations were to start at once, but the attack would not be made before 7 June.[52] Another order on the 4th explained:[52] "Corps Conta, which is charged with the protection of the left flank of the 7th Army...is compelled to temporarily assume the defensive, after positions most suitable for this purpose are captured....The offensive spirit

---

[51] The 197th Division was relieved on 7-8 June by the 5th Guard Division, a first class unit which had had special training in open warfare, preparatory to its participation in the Somme offensive (SOI 60, 8-9 Jun).

The 237th Division was relieved on 9-10 June by the 28th Division, a crack outfit which had been in the Somme battle and in the Aisne offensive of 27 May. It had been temporarily relieved by the 231st Division (see below) when it reached the Marne on 30 May (Info preceding SOI 56, 4-5 Jun). The principal elements of the 28th Division were reportedly relieved on 19-20 June by the 87th Division (SOI 72, 20-21 Jun). The 87th Division was relieved on 4-5 July by the 4th Ersatz Division (SOI 86, 4-5 Jul). Note: The relief of the 28th begun on 19-20, was cancelled three days later and the division returned to the line. The most important German division in this narrative, the 28th, comprised a single brigade, the 55th, whose units were the 40th Fusilier Regiment, 109th and 110th Grenadier Regiments, the 14th Field Artillery, and the 55th Foot (heavy) Artillery Battalion.

The 10th Reserve Division was relieved about 15 June by the 231st Division (Div Order, 231st Inf, 6 Jun, War Diaries 4).

The 231st Division, most of it opposite the French to the right of the 2nd Div on 4 June, was partially relieved on 12-13 June by elements of the 36th Division. The entire 231st was relieved on 18-19 June by the 201st Division (SOI 76, 24-25 Jun).

[52] Opns Order 515 (231st Inf, WD Annex 2, War Diaries 4).

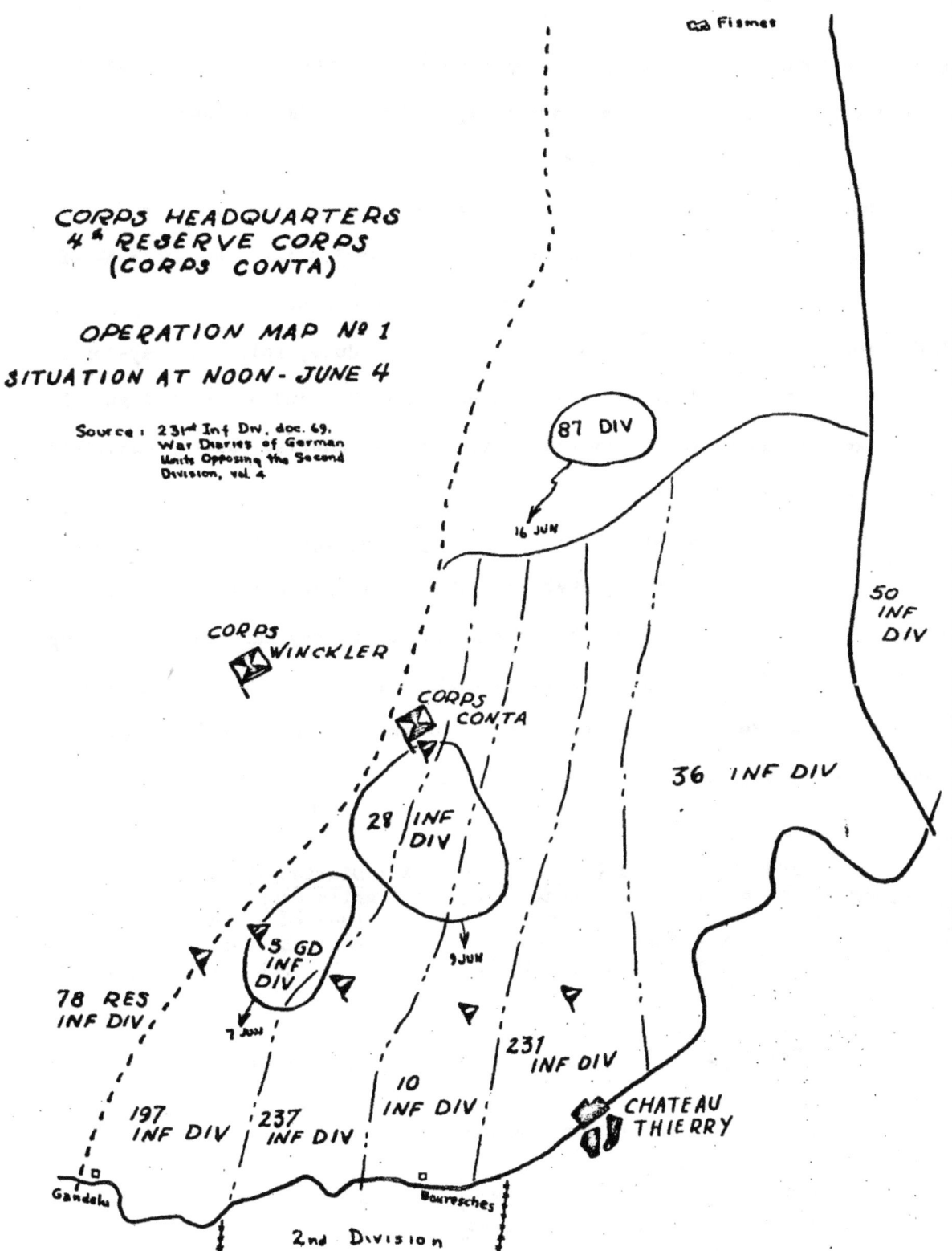

must be maintained even though a temporary lull in the attack seems to exist. In the general picture of the operations, no halt or lull exists. We are the victors and will remain on the offensive. The enemy is defeated."[53]

Meanwhile, at noon on 3 June, German artillery began firing a 7-hour bombardment of blue cross (diphenychlorarsine) shells into the woods NW of Lucy le Bocage, where some 800 Marines and Engineers were setting up positions. There were 35 casualties.[54] The next evening, 4 June, following day-long shelling of the 2nd Division area with shrapnel, HE, and occasional gas, Lucy le Bocage was hit with a short bombardment of gas shells, causing casualties of one officer and 19 men.[55]

For several days both sides were engaged in organizing their forces, preparing positions, and getting what rest they could for the fight ahead. On 5 June, incoming 150s indicated that the German artillery had been brought up, and the 23rd Infantry, rejoining the division on the line Triangle Ferme-Paris road, was subjected to the shelling of the heavies, including some yperite, as it dug in.[56]

---

[53] Corps Order 518, 4 Jun (4th Res Corps, War Diaries 1). Corps Conta was to expand to the southwest as flank protection, while Corps Winckler, Wichura, Larisch, and Francois, on its right, were to continue advancing west to reach Compiegne and eliminate the Noyon salient. Monograph, Lt Col Ernst Otto, The Fighting for Belleau Wood in June, 1918, Reichsarchiv, Potsdam, 1918, pp. 2-3 (2nd Div Box 31, 33.9).

[54] Rpt on Gas Attack, serial 10, 3 Jun (GAF-2A); Spencer, I. 113.

[55] SOI 56, 4-5 Jun; Rpt of Opns, 5 Jun.

[56] Rpt, CG 3rd Brig to CG 2nd Div, 16 Aug 18, sub: Rpt of action of 3rd Brig, June 1st to July 15th (3rd Brig, Records 6).

At 5:00 a.m. on 6 June, unaware of Corps Conta plans for attack the next day,[57] the 2nd Division, in conjunction with the 167th French Division on its left, went on the offensive, attacking without special artillery preparation[58] the objective line Hill 126-Torcy-Chateau Belleau-Bois de Belleau-Bouresches. Several objectives, including the crests overlooking Bussaires and Torcy, were reported reached that day, but not the principal objectives, the Bois de Belleau and Bouresches.[59]

On the night preceding the attack, 2,000 shells, with some yellow cross, had been fired into 2nd Division positions west of the Bois de la Marette, and in the reprisal for the attack the next day, 2,200 rounds including several bursts of mustard and lachrimatory gas shells, pounded the edge of the Bois de la Marette and the roads in the forward zone. Continuing the attack on the afternoon of the 6th, 2nd Division forces encountered intense machine gun fire, particularly in the Bois de Belleau, and both sides suffered severely in the German counterattacks that followed. Bouresches was reported captured, but the advance into Belleau Wood, where the undergrowth, rock formations, and boulders in its great ravine bristled with machine gun nests, was stopped

---

[57] "The Intelligence Service at that time had not been organized or trained for open warfare and...almost nothing was known of the composition or situation of the enemy's forces; even the location of our lines was imperfectly understood." (MS hist, The Second Division at Chateau Thierry, p. 28, 2nd Div Box 8).

[58] MS Hist of 2nd FA Brig, p. 7, says the reason was complete lack of coordination between infantry and artillery.

[59] FO 8, 2nd Div, 5 Jun; SOI 57, 5-6 Jun.

after several hundred yards.[60] Between 11:00 p.m. and 3:00 a.m. on 6-7 June, over 300 150mm palite (trichlormethyl chlorformate) and chlorpicrin shells were fired on 23rd Infantry troops in the Bois des Clerembauts, resulting in 14 light casualties, and from 9:30 p.m., 6 June, to 10 p.m., 8 June, intermittent surprise volleys of blue cross shell (diphenychlorarsine) amid continuous HE fire, produced 32 gas casualties in the 9th Infantry.[61]

A recommendation for citation offers a different account of the 23rd Infantry gas casualties. A company commander, "attempting to go into position /⎺on the night of 6-7 June_/ was caught in a very heavy gas attack, which eliminated 170 men /⎺and_/ killed one of his officers....He was seriously gassed, rendered partially blind and unable to speak," but remained with his company and consolidated his advance position.[62]

Of this two-day attack, in which 2nd Division casualties were estimated at 30 officers and 900 men killed and wounded, a German communique said: "Stubborn and not afraid of his losses the enemy pursued his useless struggle northwest of Chateau Thierry." Although repeated German counterattacks on Bouresches were said to have been repulsed, not until 10 June were the Germans finally cleared out of the railroad station so the village could be included in the new line, Hill 142-Lucy le Bocage-Triangle-southern edge of the Bois de

---

[60] SOI 58, 6-7 Jun; Jnl O, 6 Jun.

[61] Rpt of Gas Attack, ser 11 (GAF-2A); Spencer, I, 117-119. According to Ernst Otto, p. 15, the gas on 7 Jun backfired: "3 officers and 20 men /⎺became_/ sick from gas - they had swallowed German gas."

[62] Ltr, Malone CO 23rd Inf to CG 3rd Brig, 2 Jul, sub: Opns of 23rd Inf, 1 Jul (2nd Div Box 62, 33.6).

la Marette.[63]

For the next two or three days and nights following the action of 6-7 June, the 2nd Division was subjected to steady, heavy shelling on the wooded areas in its sector. On the 7th, after several 210mm shells fell nearby, division headquarters was moved from Monteuil-aux-Lions to Genevrois Farm. Through its French reconnaissance planes and reconnaissance patrols, the division learned that the German forces had begun to consolidate their positions with trenches and barbed wire entanglements, leading Intelligence to infer that Corps Conta was giving up for the time being further thought of maneuver.[64]

"The 2nd American Division, which made the attack on the evening of June 6 and that of last night," said a 28th Division report on June 8, "is probably no longer very efficient." The attacks, it went on, were obviously intended only to immobilize German forces, make local improvements in the line, and give the Americans an opportunity for headlines. "Should the Americans on our front gain the upper hand only temporarily, this may have the most unfavorable influence on the morale of the Entente and on the continuation of the war....The renewed employment of the 5th Guard and 28th Infantry Divisions on the front line of the Conta Corps is to be considered

---

[63]
War Diary, 7-10 Jun; Rpt of Opn, 8 Jun; Div Info Bul following SOI 63.
Up to midnight, 5 Jun, the 2nd Div had taken between 100-200 casualties. In the fighting from 6-8 June, 1177 wounded were evacuated, and 800-900 replacements came in on 9 June, with more on the way. Memo, Grant GHQ AEF G-3 to CofS, 12 Jun, sub: Rpt on the Condition of the 2nd Div (2nd Div Box 30, 33.6).
Ernst Otto, p. 14, says 237th Div casualties on 6 Jun were 6 officers and 72 men killed, 10 officers and 218 men wounded, 5 officers and 90 men missing. In the 10th Div, 24 men were killed, 101 men wounded, 2 officers and 24 men missing -- a total of 552 battle casualties.

[64]
SOI 60, 62, 64.

from this point of view."[65]

3rd Division Intelligence reported that same day that these two crack German divisions, the 5th and 28th, were coming into the line opposite the 2nd Division, their mission an offensive that would break through the 2nd, with Meaux its objective. A prisoner captured the next day confirmed the relief and said the attack would be made "in two or three days and they were going to use lots of gas."[66] But the 2nd Division had its own plans.

On 7-8 June, it began concentrating machine gun and artillery fire and marshalling its forces for an assault on Belleau Wood. Beginning about 3:30 a.m. on the 10th, the batteries of the division, with their French support, fired a total of 28,000 rounds of 77mm's and 12,000 155mm's into the 300 acres of tangled woods and rocky ravines of the Bois de Belleau. In the attack in the dense fog at dawn, the Marine brigade advanced 800 meters on a two-kilometer front (approximately on a line through Hill 169), against elements of the 28th Division coming in to relieve the 10th Division and a unit of the 237th in the wood.[67]

On several occasions prior to this assault, that is, on the night of 6-7 June and the morning of 9 June, the German battalion at Torcy reported that tear gas and other unidentified gas shells fell on them. The reports

---

[65] Daily Rpt, 28th Div (Item 164, 1st Annex, War Diaries 2).

[66] FM fr G-2 3rd Div, 8 Jun (Records 4); FM G-2, 10:10 p.m., 9 Jun.

[67] FO 3, 4th Brig, 6:30 p.m., 9 Jun (Records 4); SOI 61, 9-10 Jun; Rpt, Opns of 2nd FA Brig, 30 May-25 Jun (Records 9).
The postwar Field Notes of Col John Magruder, FA, describe in detail the terrain of the Bois de Belleau (2nd Div Box 9, 18.8).

- 26 -

of the same unit for 10, 13, and 14 June agreed that "the enemy frequently fires gas shells." Since the 2nd Division records no use of gas during this period, it must be presumed that the gas was fired by the neighboring French unit or by the artillery attached to the Division.[68]

Either in retaliation for the French gas or to harass possible reinforcements for the Marines in the wood, between 9:30 a.m. and 2:45 p.m. on 11 June, from 150 to 250 77mm and 105mm blue cross shells were fired on 23rd Infantry troops in the Bois des Clerembauts. Only seven men were reported gassed, when a shell burst directly over their dugout.[69] That same day, the 11th, after further artillery preparation and preceded by a rolling barrage, the Marine brigade attacked the northern half of the Bois de Belleau and reportedly occupied the entire wood, capturing more than 450 prisoners, 30 machine guns, and 4 minenwerfers or trench mortars. Positions in the wood were said to have been consolidated and remaining machine gun nests cleaned up that night, with the capture of 43 additional prisoners. A German gas bombardment of Bouresches on the night of 11-12 June seems not to have been reported in 2nd Division records.[70]

Actually, the Marine action was filled with confusion, leading to confused reports, for the main German defense line at the top of the wood remained

---

[68] See Combat Rpt, 1st Bn, 460th Inf (doc 83, War Diaries 4).

[69] Rpt of Gas Attack, ser. 14, 12 Jun; Spencer, I. 120.

[70] SOI 62, 63, 64, 10-13 Jun; Rpt of Opns, 11-12 Jun. See note below for gassing of Bouresches.

intact. Beginning on 12 June, German forces were seen filtering back into the wood on the western edge, where they set up machine gun strong points to harass the patrols sent against them. It was estimated that in the next ten days German forces in battalion strength, with 75 to 100 machine guns, had returned to the woods.[71] The 2nd Division held the southern half of the wood but could not claim possession of the northern sector.

Achievement of the new line, reported in the divisional War Diary for 11 June as Hill 142-northern edge of Bois de Belleau-Bouresches-Triangle-Bois des Clerambauts-north of Monneaux, had been costly. Total casualties from 1-12 June were said to be 321 killed, with 2,958 wounded evacuated through Meaux.[72] The gassed were presumably included with the wounded. The Germans were aware of the cost through their interrogation of the 5th Marine prisoners, who told them that "Casualties during the attack, and during the last few days by heavy artillery, considerably high, allegedly 30 or 40% in the 5th Regiment....Gas bombardment on Bouresches in the night of June 11-12 caused a few casualties despite the fact that the men were immediately warned by specially trained gas officers, and adjusted their masks."[73]

But the toll in combat fatigue was still higher. A telegram from General Bundy to Pershing on 10 June asked for an infantry brigade to relieve weary units of the 2nd Division, all of whose regiments were in the line and

---

[71] Rpt, 2nd FA Brig to G-3, sub: Movements from 31 May to 10 Jul (Records 6).

[72] War Diary, 12 Jun; FM fr Hq Fld Hosp Sec, 14 Jun, said evacuated wounded from 3-12 Jun totaled 2,355.

[73] 5th Guard Div, Interr Rpt, 13 Jun (Item 213, 2nd Gd Inf Brig, (War Diaries 3).

had been continuously "moving, marching, entrenching and fighting since May 30th." On the 11th, Harbord said of his 4th Marine Brigade in Belleau: "Officers and men are now in a state scarcely less than complete physical exhaustion."[74] Indicative as much of the physical condition of 2nd Division troops as of inexperience was the incident of the company of 2nd Engineers who ran into a heavy barrage of mixed HE, smoke, mustard gas on its way through the Bois de Belleau on the afternoon of the 12th to reinforce the Marines in the line. Two officers and 24 men in the company were killed or wounded, an unidentified number overcome by gas. "Out of the company of 185, only about 50 men arrived at their objective," the remainder not gassed or wounded becoming lost, "not being able to travel through thick woods and underbrush in gas masks." The company was withdrawn early on the morning of the 14th when it again encountered gas in the wood.[75]

---

[74] Tele, 2nd Div, 10 Jun; Rpt 4th Brig to CG 2nd Div, 8:00 a.m., 11 Jun (Records 6).
The necessity for relief was questioned since it was expected that "This part of the front would soon become a quiet sector," said memo Lt Col W. S. Grant, GHQ AEF G-3 for CofS, 12 Jun, sub: Rpt on Condition of 2nd Div, and atchd corresp (2nd Div Box 30, 33.6).

[75] Rpt of Co F, 2nd Eng, 11-14 Jun (Records 7); Rpt on Gas Attack, ser. 12, and Spencer, I. 121, say the company was surprised by blue cross, causing 10 gas casualties. Hanslian, p. 96, says the number of shells may not have been large, but Harbord, in the Diary of the 4th Brig, 30 May-30 Jun, p. 42 (2nd Div Box 4, 11.5), reports "Considerable gas used on the Bois de Belleau and on the Torcy front" on the 12th.

The Gas Attack of 13-14 June

Delayed in its plans by the American attacks, Corps Conta initiated new preparations on 11 June for its operation "to improve our position and inflict damage on the Americans." In the assault, the 28th Division was to move down against Bouresches and Hill 201, the newly arrived 195th Division was to drive between the Bois des Clerembauts and Bois de la Marette, with the 36th and 231st Divisions advancing in support of the right flank down the Marne bank to the Bois du Loup and Essomes.[76] To protect their flank in this move, the Germans had first to recapture the Bois de Belleau, so cheaply won from the French and now in part so dearly lost to the 2nd Division.

At 4:15 on 12 June, after a 15-minute surprise fire by its artillery, a battalion of the 110th Grenadiers, 28th Division, attacked the southern part of the Bois de Belleau and occupied its former positions there, only to be evicted late that afternoon by Marine patrols. The grenadiers reported the ravine between the wood and Hill 190 under continual gas shelling by the artillery.[77] The 28th Division order said that night: "The Bois de Belleau and Bouresches will be captured on June 13th at 4:10 a.m." This was to be accomplished after a 10-minute surprise bombardment with gas and HE by U. S. artillery of three divisions, to be followed by a rolling barrage for the attack.[78]

---

[76] Corps Order, Opns No. 557, 6:30 P.M., 11 Jun (Item 222, 4th Res Corps, War Diaries 1).

[77] War Diary of 110th Gren, 12 Jun (War Diaries 3).

[78] Div Order 1394, 28th Div, 10:40 p.m., 12 Jun (Item 200, 2nd Annex, War Diaries 2).

The hostile massed fire with "much gas" that was laid on the Bois and its roads of approach fell on the positions of both brigades, the irritating gas and yperite "giving [the Marines in the wood, particularly] a lot of trouble."[79] The divisional artillery, alerted to enemy intentions, replied with a heavy barrage on the 28th Division forces massed along the railroad embankment east of Belleau Wood. Subsequently, German reports said that "between 3:00 and 5:00 a.m. [there was] vigorous shelling of Rochet Wood with gas," as the Torcy area came "under most intense artillery fire. Enemy again makes extravagant use of gas shells. It is an attempt to block an operation of the 461st Infantry [237th Division] in Belleau Wood."[80]

Thrown off balance, the 28th Division attacked the town of Bouresches on the line Belleau-Bouresches sometime after 4:00 a.m. After several hours of heavy fighting, the German forces withdrew. The 2nd Division had suffered only "moderate losses" (i.e., approximately 600 killed and wounded).[81] At 9:30 a.m. on 13 June, with the failure of the 28th to advance, the general attack by Corps Conta was called off. Bitter recriminations were heaped on

---

[79] SOI 64, 12-13 June; Morning Rpt, Arty Comdr, 237th Div, 13 Jun (doc 78, War Diaries 4). The Rpt of Gas Attack, ser. 15, 14 Jun, said there were 14 blue cross casualties in the 23rd Inf that night, caused by surprise, exhaustion, and early removal of masks. A telegram from Bundy to C Gas Serv, 14 Jun, said yellow and blue cross shelling of 9th Inf near Triangle had resulted in 40 casualties. The Rpt of Gas Attack, ser. 16, corrected this to 59 gas cases in the 9th Inf, resulting from too early removal of mask and delayed evacuation.

[80] Intel Bul, 231st Div, 12-13 Jun (Item 145, doc 71, War Diaries 4); War Diary of 460th Inf, 2:30-4:00 a.m., 13 Jun (doc 82, War Diaries 4).

[81] SOI 64, 12-13 Jun; Rpt of Opns, 13 Jun; FM fr CO 4th Brig, 5:35 a.m., 13 Jun.

the division for its "refusal" to move off the Belleau-Bouresches road.[82]

That day the Germans reported blocking fire and a small number of gas shells ("a sweet odor and caused sneezing") on Torcy and Hill 126.[83] At 9:50 p.m. that night, the Germans admitted: "Emeny has captured Bois de Belleau. The wood will be kept under HE and gas the whole night. Wood will be recaptured 14 June." The same night, 13-14 June, refused permission by the French to shorten his front and unable to get brigade or division relief, General Bundy arranged to shorten the line held by the Marines by transferring the Bouresches sector to the 23rd Infantry.[84] The 5th Marine battalion that had occupied that village in the hollow was moved back to Lucy le Bocage to rest in brigade reserve. The 6th Marine battalion in reserve at Lucy then set out to relieve another 5th Marine battalion in the Bois de Belleau.

The "first gas bombardment of any size since coming into the sector" commenced about midnight of 13 June when Lucy le Bocage and the southern half of the Bois de Belleau were "saturated" with between 6,000 and 7,000 rounds of yellow cross (Map No. 5). The intention was to "cut off the territory

---

[82] Message, 244th Brig to 237th Div (Item 148, doc 79); message, Bischoff, CO 461st Regt, 237th Div to 244th Brig, 17 Jun (Item 158-60, doc 79, War Diaries 4).

[83] Regtl Gas O to Div Gas O, 1:15 p.m., 13 Jun (Item 206, doc 82, 460th Inf, 237th Div, War Diaries 4).

[84] FM to 40th Fusiliers; FM to 83rd FA (Item 162, doc 79, 237th Div, War Diaries 4). Ltr, Grant to Fox Conner GHQ AEF G-3, 13 June, no sub (2nd Div Box 30, 33.6).

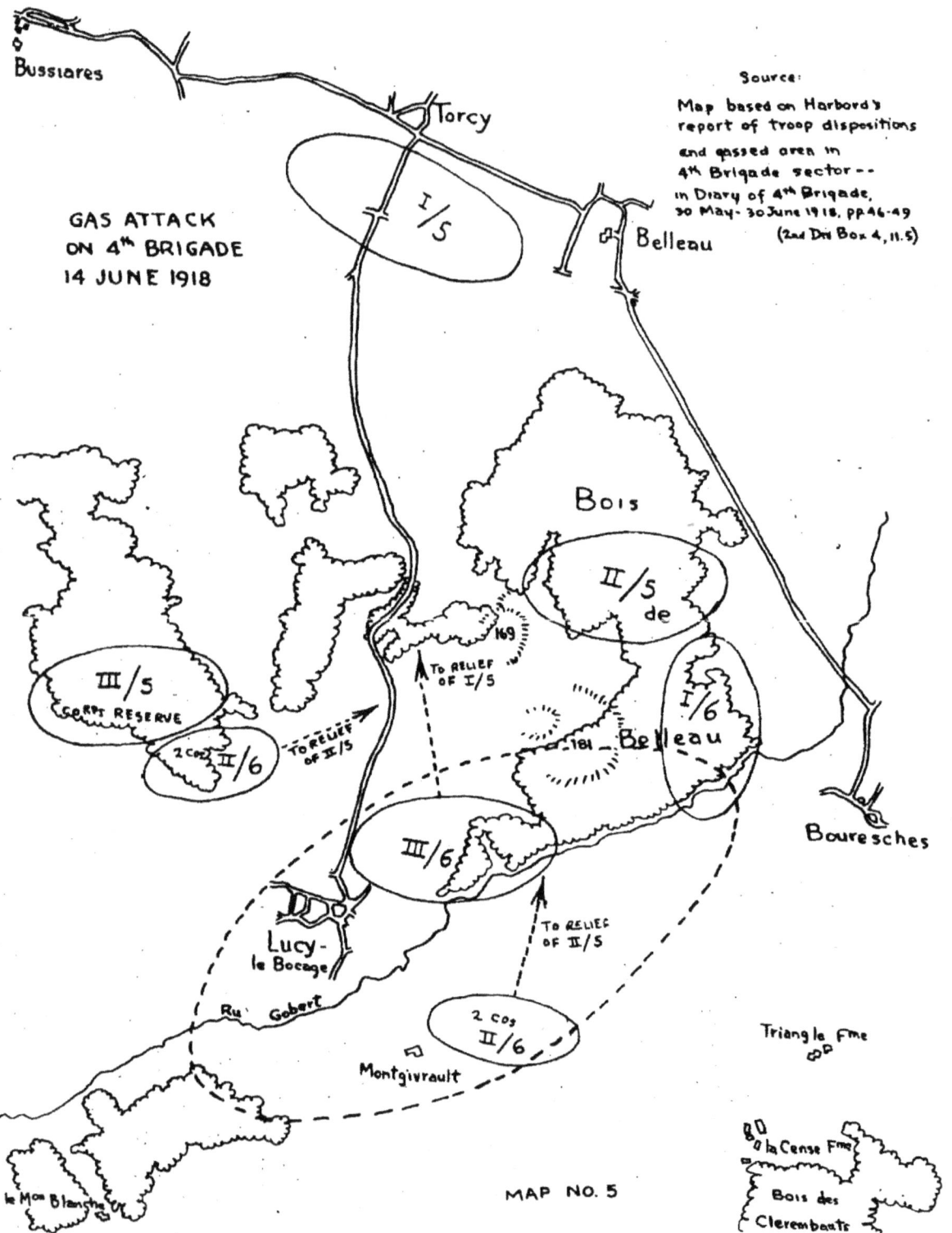

likely to be used in advancing against Belleau Wood."[85] A German report of the attack said: "At night drenching bombardment (yellow cross) on south part of Belleau Woods, and vicinity of Lucy le Bocage, harassing fire on Domptin." And in the noon report on the 14th: "Batteries continue harassing fire on Bois de Belleau and Bouresches and completed the drenching bombardment with yellow cross on Lucy and the depression...with a 2-hour follow-up gas bombardment."[86]

At 3:45 a.m. on the 14th, the 3rd Battalion, 6th Marines, on its way from Lucy to the Bois, to relieve a unit of the 5th Marines, reported: "Gas attack on woods E of Lucy entire ravine E of Lucy and sector of front line entering Bouresches and Triangle Farm very serious. Men have had on respirators 5½ hours. Suggest men be moved from infected area. Mustard gas is being used. Request Division Gas Officer. (FM F-13 to CO 6th Mar, Records 5)." Two hours later a message from the 6th Marine commander to the Regimental Aid Station said: "Succeeded in getting through message to Division Gas Officer about situation with order 600 complete suits...1st Bn just reported all companies under fairly heavy gas shelling, masks on & OK. (FM 5:35 a.m. 14 Jun.)" At 6:03 a.m., the commander reported to his brigade that 270 men had

---

[85]
 Corps Conta order, cited by Hanslian, p. 98, also shows that 3625 yellow cross had been made available to the 237th Div arty and 4650 yellow cross rounds to the 28th Div arty. The arty order of the 28th Div (Hanslian, p. 99) said the 237th Div arty would put 2415 rounds on Lucy and the valley behind Bouresches, the 28th Div arty to fire 4550 rounds into the hollow S and SE of Bouresches. Four-fifths of the shell was to be fired in one-hour bombardments, the remainder in a two-hour follow up fire.
 The 237th Div arty comdr reported firing 2623 rounds of yellow cross betw 12:00 and 6:00 a.m. (doc 78, 237th Div, War Diaries 4). There is no rpt available from the 28th Div arty comdr.
 Hanslian (p. 97) reports a total of only 1725 rounds of yellow cross actually fired in this opn. SOI 65, 13-14 Jun, estimates 1500 yperite shell.

[86]
 Daily Rpt, 13-14 Jun, 28th Div (2nd Annex, War Diaries 2).

- 33 -

been taken to the aid station at Hill 201. Two men were found badly gassed, 38 moderately, 120 very slightly.

Instructions were given to keep them out of blankets and open their clothes, to avoid burning cases of saturated clothing. Lt. Taylor reports that a company of the 23rd Inf moving to relief last night were badly shot up and in need of medical attention. Lt. Chandler, Regtl Gas Officer, was sent to the area /‾south of Belleau Wood_/ and reports that he found from 50 to 60 men...more or less gassed through removing respirators to attend to their wounds.

The 6th Marine Regimental Surgeon said at 10:40 a.m.: "75 to 150 men evacuated since arrival this morning. Practically entire battalion physically unfit due to gas. Immediate measures should be taken to secure relief of this battalion due to a generalized gassing. Evacuation still continues. Battalion now camped in gassed area." Reporting later on the event, the 5th Marine unit that was waiting relief and was itself suffering gas casualties at the time, said of the ill-fated battalion: "2nd Battalion, 6th Marines were badly gassed and instead of arriving night 13-14 with about 800 men only 325 effectives arrived, so that attack could not be delivered, and I did not consider that they were sufficient to relieve me and remained in position."[87]

Harbord in a message to Bundy at 4:00 p.m. on the 14th apparently knew only that at least 225 men in two companies of the 6th Marines had been gassed and evacuated that day. In his War Diary entry later that evening, however, he reported 563 gas casualties in the 1st and 2nd Battalions of that Marine regiment.[88] But Colonel Grant, on the G-3 staff, GHQ, wrote to Fox

---

[87] Rpt of Opns, 2nd Bn, 5th Mar, 2-16 Jun (Records 7).

[88] FM CG 4th Brig to CG 2nd Div; War Diary, Records 6.
Spencer, I.126, cites a telegram from Bundy to the Gas Service at Tours on 14 Jun reporting 700 yellow and blue cross casualties in the 6th Marines and 23rd Inf in wood NE of Lucy, with gas attack continuing.

Conner from 2nd Division headquarters after the gas attack: "Night of June 13-14 passed quietly. Troops were able to get some rest. Gen. Bundy, Colonel Brown and General Harbord all seemed to feel better, and need of relief did not seem so great as it had 48 or even 24 hours before." Then, a paragraph later:

> Meanwhile the Germans put down on our front lines and on rear areas, intermittently during the day and evening, a heavy gas bombardment, paying particular attention to the Bois de Belleau.....At 10:45 p.m., June 14, gas casualties were reported as between 700 and 800, the Marines being greatest sufferers. Cases were mostly burns with some severe cases. Medical officer reported that practically none of the gassed would be available for duty for at least two weeks.[89]

The Germans intended this gas to interdict the approach to Belleau Wood and the wood itself, and so facilitate their advance to the defensive line they had selected north of the Paris road. Yet despite observed circulation of men and caissons in the German back area, Intelligence said of the gassing: "From the indiscriminate use of mustard gas it would appear that the object of the enemy is merely to cause losses and not to prepare for immediate attack."[90] Colonel Grant, in his letter of the 15th, said that "Hq. VIth Army believe that the gas bombardment in connection with massing of German batteries in this region indicates a German attack in a few days. It

---

[89] Ltr, Lt Col Grant to Conner, GHQ G-3, 15 Jun (2nd Div Box 30).

[90] SOI 65, 13-14 Jun. 2nd Div Intelligence, in an Estimate of the Enemy Situation, 10:00 p.m., 14 Jun (2nd Div Box 12), said of the German 7th Army movements that the weight of the main effort for the next few days would still be from the north in the direction of Compiegne and from the east in the direction of Villers-Cotterets. On the 2nd Div front, the enemy effort was likely to be purely defensive except to improve lines and inflict losses. No serious intent to regain the Bois de Belleau was probable, and reported shelling of the wood and Bouresches with mustard gas further indicated that the enemy had no intention of action in that area.
On 14 Jun, according to Ernst Otto, p. 30, the German High Command ordered the Army Group of the Crown Prince to assume the defensive, discontinuing the 18th Army atk at Noyon and the 7th Army atk W and SW of Soissons.

is highly probable that until gas is dissipated no infantry attack need be feared."

The bombardment continued on the 14th when about 4:30 p.m. the Bois de Belleau was again hit with yperite. At 5:37 p.m. the 6th Marines reported to Harbord that gas was still falling: "Weak concentration mustard gas. Long exposure. Men have worn masks about 6 hours and some have taken them off... Hughes says his orders are to stick it out...Gas Officer advocated movement higher ground...Regtl Surgeon reports 185 evacuations 1st Bn (FM to CG 4th Brig, 14 Jun)." Then between 9:30 p.m. and 12:30 a.m. on the 14-15 June between 4:00 and 6:00 a.m. the Bois de Belleau, as well as La Voie du Chatel, Lucy le Bocage, Montgivrault, and Domptin were subjected to heavy gas concentrations, the result of an estimated 500 105mm gas shells. At 1:30 on the morning of the 15th, three companies of the 23rd Infantry, on their way to relieve a Marine battalion in Belleau Wood, were bombarded with HE and shrapnel and then 350 77mm and 105mm rounds of yellow and blue cross gas. Two of the companies moved out of the gassed ravine they were in; the third met a Marine company, and when the bombardment ceased, were told by its captain that it was safe to remove their masks. At least 150 men in the infantry company were evacuated that evening.[91]

At 8:00 a.m. on 15 June, Harbord was at last able to withdraw his troops from the woods to Hills 169 and 181 nearby, and asked the 23rd Infantry in Bouresches to cover the eastern edge of the Bois with machine gun support for him.[92] This was done. A suggestion to Malone of the 23rd Infantry that he move

---

[91] Rpt of Gas Attack, ser. 17, 16 Jun; Spencer, I, 127; Hanslian, p. 100.

[92] FM CG 4th Brig to CG 3rd Brig.

reserves into Bouresches to replace his forces covering the Bois was turned down. "It is unwise to put more troops in Bouresches. Our main line will cross from the vicinity of Triangle towards 181 where the right of main line of Marines will probably rest....Am arranging for gas against all the approaches to Bouresches and for strong harassing fire in the same areas (FM to CO 3rd Bn, 10:55 a.m., 15 Jun; FM 8:55 p.m., Records 5, 23rd Inf)."

The renewed gassing of the Bois de Belleau in the early morning of the 15th resulted, an enemy report said, when the Germans became alarmed by sudden intense machine gun fire on their front lines. However, the gas backfired on the Germans, as they admitted: "This gas was quite bothersome in our own lines."[93] It is possible this backfire was a contributory reason for the "half-hearted" German attack made along the northern edge of the Bois and down past Bouresches on the night of 15 June. Driven back, a second attack was made at 4:45 a.m. and again broken up, principally by artillery fire.[94]

The count of the gas casualties in the two-day bombardment came in slowly. Up to noon on the 14th, 420 casualties had been reported, the greater number of these Marine and 23rd Infantry cases, "most of them badly burned about the body."[95] By 11:00 p.m. that night, almost 700 casualties, some very severe, had been evacuated, and evacuations were not yet complete.[96] By the

---

[93] Combat Rpt, 1st Bn, 2nd Baden Gren Brig (110th Gren Regt, War Diaries 3).

[94] SOI 67, 15-16 Jun; Jnl O, 15 Jun.

[95] Rpt of Opns, 14 Jun; FM fr Div Surg, 10 a.m., 14 Jun, Jnl O, 14 Jun.

[96] Jnl O, 14 Jun.

morning of 15 June, total casualties reported as admitted on the previous day to the gas hospital at Luzancy were 745 due to gas, 16 shell shock, and 10 gassed and wounded.[97] The Medical Director of the Gas Service later reported a total of "over 800 cases."[98]

Reprisal and Stalemate

A 2nd Division telegram to Pershing on the events of 15-16 June said that following the gas attacks, enemy artillery continued harassing "our front line and back area using much gas," while "our artillery replied with harassing fire using some gas."[99] The Operations Report of the 2nd F.A. Brigade was to say: "The division was considerably handicapped as the enemy seemed to have plenty of gas /shells_/ while our artillery had very few."[100] No mention is made of mustard gas shell, the cause of most of the Division's gas casualties. Yet the French were at last producing yperite in quantity (a considerably more toxic product than German mustard gas) and it was coming into the field. On 15 June, General Naulin, the new commander of the XXI French Army Corps, replacing Degoutte, wrote to the Commanding General of the 6th French Army:

---

[97] Rpt of Opns, 15 Jun; FM fr Div Surg, 9:20 a.m., 15 Jun; Jnl O, 15 Jun, reported 771 casualties up to 6:00 a.m. that date.

[98] Ltr to C Gas Serv AEF, 1 Jul 18, sub: Rpt of Second Serious Gas Attack on 2nd Div (GAF-2S). Note: The gas discipline of the troops in this attack is reported in the Analysis below.
The Division Surgeon was later to say that the attack of the 14th necessitated "the evacuation of over 900 members of the 2nd Bn, 6th Marines." (Richard Derby, Wade In, Sanitary! NY: G. P. Putnam, 1919, p. 72).

[99] Cf. Diary of 4th Brig, 3 Jun (2nd Div Box 4, 11.5). Jnl O, 16 Jun; and ltr Lt Col Grant, GHQ G-3 (at 2nd Div Hq) to Col Fox Conner, GHQ G-3, 18 Jun (2nd Div Box 30), on French economy of ammo.

[100] A German confirmation of the inequality seems to appear on Combat Rpt, 3rd Bn, 110th Gren Regt (War Diaries 3) where for the period 18-30 Jun it is said: "Our own and the enemy artillery fought one another quite intensely; the former employing blue and yellow cross gas shells against enemy artillery firing positions and camps. On an average, the firing lasted 2 hrs."

I have the honor to draw your attention to the necessity that some measures be taken to reply effectively to the yperite bombardment which the enemy has just effected on the 2nd U.S. Division and which he seems to wish to continue.

The best means seems to be to reply to this type of attack by similar means.

Consequently I have the honor to ask you that some yperite shells in sufficient quantity be placed at my disposal to be employed on the known enemy positions in front of us (in particular, woods and bottoms of valleys).

If, as I have heard it said, the lots of yperite munitions are ready, I most urgently ask you to assign some to me in view of the severity of the attack which the American units have just been subjected to, and which continues today.[101]

The next day, in a Service Note to the artillery (presumably, both French and American units), General Naulin said that his request for 75mm yperite shell would probably be granted. When it arrived he would order its use "in immediate reprisal," in a barrage on enemy troops in the ravine to the north of Brusses, to the south of Givry, and to the northeast of Belleau, including the villages there.

On the 17th, the order for reprisal was issued, to be "executed by the Artillery of the 2nd I.D.U.S." A total of 5,900 rounds would be fired in a three-hour bombardment, mixed with 2,200 75mm and 155mm HE rounds, on four targets in the ravine from north of Brusses Ferme to south of Givry and in the area northwest of Bois de Belleau. The yperite shells would be drawn from the depot at Davids and issued to the seven batteries of the 2nd F.A. Brigade in position for the designated objectives. The bombardment would begin on telephone order of the XXI Army Corps.[102]

Records of the 2nd F.A. do not show receipt of this yperite, but that it was received at some time after the 17th is clear, since approximately

---

[101] Translation from copy in fol. 21st AC, Vol. II, p. 64 (French Files Box 95). See CWS Intel Bul G-12, 11 Jul, for transl of Petain's circular of 29 May on the use of the new yperite shells.

[102] 21st Corps d'Armee Order, 17 June (2nd Div Box 25, 32.7). Also in 21st AC file above, pp. 68-70.

this allotment of yperite was fired on 1 July, in the attack on Vaux. A sentence in General Naulin's order of the 17th suggests why it was not fired at once: "This fire not being executed except as immediate reprisal for an enemy yperite shoot, immediate notice will be given to the General Staff of the 21st A.C. of all bombardment made by the Germans with this gas."

Meanwhile, the divisional artillery fired what gas it had, "As a retaliatory measure for gas thrown on the Bois de Belleau," said the War Diary for the 14th, "the 12th FA has been asked to gas the village of Givry and the deep ravine...between Givry and Bouresches....The 17th FA was also asked to put some heavy shells into Torcy and the Chateau Belleau."[103] Early on 15 June, "4,000 #19 gas shells were fired into the Bois de Rochets,"[104] as reprisal for gassing Lucy le Bocage. It caused, German prisoners later said, over 400 casualties.[105]

In answer to Col. Malone's request of the 15th for gas, the 15th F.A. replied: "100 gas to NE Bouresches are on the way. We are using tonight over 1,000 gas shells (cyanogen) on Boche woods opposite our area. If there is any

---

103
    A postwar report by the 12th FA said it fired no gas at Chateau Thierry (see Analysis, below).

104
    Note this target is nowhere near Naulin's designations. Moreover, there was no French gas designated #19. It may have been #9, martonite (bromacetone), or considering the quantity, #4, Vincennite (cyanogen), which the French disposed of to American artillery, since it was not considered an effective shell. "The use of Vincennite is being abandoned by all belligerents, but at the present time it is still used by the French, who occasionally turn such shells over to American Troops." (Pamphlet, Provisional Instructions for Artillery Officers on the Use of Gas Shell, CGO 1st Army, 1 Oct 1918, p. 5, WD Hist Box 300).
    For comment on "a serious thing, this No. 9," see Message CofS 2nd Div to CofS 5th C, 1 Nov (2nd Div Box 27, 33, Brief of Orders).

105
    Opns of 2nd FA Brig (Records 9).

information that you can give me relative to areas in Boche front line where construction is going on, I would like to send some gas there (FM to CO 23rd Inf, Records 5, 23rd Inf)." Said a German report of this reprisal: "At night consistent harassing fire on forward positions...gas surprise fires on battery positions....Our artillery fired on rearward communications and shelters with strong surprise fires, including 500 rounds of blue cross."[106]

The relief requested by Bundy on the 10th became imperative following the gas attack of 14-15 June. Between 16-18 June, three battalions of the 7th Infantry, 3rd Division and one battalion from the 174th Infantry, French 167th Division came into the 2nd Division's sector to release the badly hurt Marine battalions for reorganization and rest.[107] A report of investigation by the Division Inspector revealed that the gas bombardment, coming on top of two weeks of steady fighting, had reduced four Marine battalions to less than half their normal strength. In the period between 1-16 June, as a result of gas and HE casualties, the three battalions of the 5th Marines had lost a total of 45 officers and 1,579 men; the 2nd Battalion, 6th Marines had lost 21 officers and 836 men; and the 1st Battalion, 23rd Infantry had lost 9 officers and 121 men -- a total of 75 officers and 2,536 men in these five battalions alone.[108]

---

[106] 2nd Morning Rpt, 28th Gren Inf Div, 10:45 a.m., 16 Jun (Item 223, 3rd Annex, War Diaries 2).

[107] Rpt of Opns, 16-18 Jun; War Diary, 18 Jun.

[108] Jnl O, 17-19 Jun. Similar statistics in Jnl O, 29 Jun, said the 3rd Bn, 5th Marines, up to that time had lost 18 officers and 776 men, while the 3rd Bn, 23rd Infantry, had lost 18 officers and 507 men. Accumulative replacement data show 100 officers and 4,539 men were received by the 2nd Div between 8 Jun-10 Jul. MS hist, p. 23 (2nd Div Box 8) and War Diary, 13 Jun-10 Jul.

The two depleted and exhausted opposing forces continued to assail one another as the 2nd Division held its line from the east base of Hill 142-north of Lucy le Bocage-Hill 169-Bouresches-Triangle-Bois des Clerembauts-north of Monneaux.[109] For the next five days enemy infantry action was neglible while the Germans clung tenaciously to the ungassed northern and eastern parts of Belleau Wood, and after two days of fierce artillery fire, including some gas shell, it too slackened off. The enemy began seriously to dig in, constructing trench-works battery emplacements, and extending his network of camouflage, while 2nd Division artillery fired destructive and harassing missions daily on enemy crossroads, battery positions, and suspected troop areas.[110]

On 16 June, Corps Conta admitted that it, as well as the attack elements of 7th Army, had been stopped cold in the drive towards Paris, when it published a 7th Army summary dated 13 June looking back to earlier successes: "The main offensive of the 7th Army, commenced on May 27, has come to an end ....The severe defeat of the opponent...is evident in the loss of all his positions, his military and civil stores, between the Aisne and Marne, as well as in the loss of about 60,000 prisoners and 830 guns....The divisions will establish and allocate themselves for the control of the area that has been won."[111]

---

[109] War Diary, 17 Jun.

[110] SOI 72, 20-21 Jun.

[111] Corps Order 631, noon, 16 Jun (Item 220, 3rd Annex, War Diaries 2).

In its reports of harassing missions, there is no record of 2nd Division artillery firing any gas shell on the night of 16-17 June, yet a 28th Division battalion combat report for the 17th said: "From evening until early morning the enemy shelled the woods occupied by the battalion continuously and profusely with gas. Several direct hits by gas shells caused considerable losses."[112] Again it may be assumed that this was a gas shoot by the French artillery with the division. In any event, retaliation was swift. From midnight to 4:00 a.m. on 17 June, 400 105mm HE and gas shells fell on the Bois des Clerembauts, while 1,200 HE and gas shells (77, 105, 150mm) struck the area of La Cense Ferme, to the left of the wood. As of 6:00 a.m. on the 17th, 71 wounded, 42 gassed, and 4 gassed and wounded had been counted.[113]

Continuing the intermittent day and night bombardment of 2nd Division positions with gas and HE, 140 gas-filled 105s were fired into the Bois de la Marette on the night of 17 June, and Marigny was bombarded with gas at 7:40 the next morning. Between 1:00 and 6:00 p.m. on 18 June, 100 HE and gas 105s fell in the Bois des Clerembauts, and between 6:00 and 11:00 p.m., 180 HE and gas-filled 77s and 105s in the Bois de la Marette again.[114] The Germans reported captured American prisoners as saying there had been "considerable casualties in the artillery located near Marigny," as well as among 2nd Division horses.[115] A flurry of reports that the Germans were again massing for an

---

[112] 2nd Bn, 110th Gren (Item 72-76, doc. 30, War Diaries 3).

[113] SOI 68, 16-17 Jun; Rpt of Opns, 17 Jun.

[114] SOI 69, 70, 17-19 Jun.

[115] Intel Bul 8, 28th Div, 26/27 Jun (Item 189, 5th Annex, War Diaries 2).

attack on the Bois de Belleau resulted in an order to the artillery to put down heavy concentrations of HE on Givry at 7:00 p.m. on the 18th, and gas on the Bois de Rochets.[116] No further details occur, nor word of the attack.

Only occasional rounds of gas shell came into the 2nd Division sector during the next several days. During the lull on 19 June, the 1st Battalion, 30th Engineers (First Gas Regiment) arrived in the sector. Its attachment to the division was apparently the result of Grant's letter of the 15th, when means of retaliation were being sought for the recent gassing:

> I have taken up matter of 2 companies of gas throwers with General Bunday (sic) and Chief of Staff, requesting that they ascertain from 21st Corps whether French desire their use on this front. No decision from Corps has been communicated to me, but Brown thinks they might be useful and I recommend they be sent.... [Note added on the 16th:] Have been waiting until after 12:00 to find out from Corps regarding use of gas throwers....no reply yet received.[117]

The First Gas Regiment took no part in the subsequent operations of the division. As a 23rd Infantry report was to say of the Regiment some time later, "The gas and flame service was omnipresent but had no opportunity to operate."[118] The Regiment itself said of its activities with the 2nd Division and, later, the 26th Division:

> Working with the 2nd and 26th American Divisions, reconnaisances were carried out by officers of Companies B and D on the sectors opposite Vaux, Bois de Belleau, Belleau Village, Bouresches, and Torcy. Project reports for gas operations were submitted for bombardment of suitable targets in these sectors, and clearance was obtained for a projector operation with emplacements near Vaux and targets in the Bois de Brulets and Bois de Rochets. Owing

---

116   Rpt, Opns of 2nd FA Brig (Records 9).

117   Ltr, Lt Col Grant, Opns Sec GS (at 2nd Div Hq) to Col Fox Conner, GHQ AEF G-3, 15 Jun (2nd Div Box 30).

118   Rpt of Opns, 1-7 Nov (Records 7).

to the receipt of orders for a general attack, this operation was cancelled by Corps.

And elsewhere:

Targets for projector operations existed and projects planned, but owing to unsettled conditions and to the changing command, clearances not obtained until a few days before the attack (i.e., the 2nd battle of the Marne, on 18 July). Cancelled at last moment, due to orders for a general advance. Gas troops used as reserves and later on road work. After 1 July, used for smoke and thermit on machine guns.[119]

Of a principal weapon of gas troops, the Stokes mortar, which by then had been converted to HE fire as well, a Marine report said: "a Stokes Mortar very useful against machine gun nests when nest is located."[120] A second Marine account contradicted this: "Stokes Mortars were carried by the battalion but no opportunity was found for their use."[121]

In the lull after the 18th, enemy aerial activity increased and sniping, machine gun fire, and artillery exchanges continued on both sides, with the principal target of the division the Bois de Belleau, its northern sector still commanded by German machine gun nests. Several attempts made by the 7th Infantry, still attached to the Division, to take these nests on 20-21 June were beaten back, but other elements of the 7th Infantry made small gains between the top of the woods and the extreme left of the Division sector.[122] On the night of 21 June, the 3rd Battalion, 6th Marines returned to the Bois de Belleau relieving one of the 7th Infantry units, and the fight for

---

[119] MS Hist of CWS AEF First Gas Regt, Pt. III, "The Chateau Thierry-Vesle Opn, Jun 30 to Sep 12," sec. 3, p. 1 (CMLHO). See also Fries and West pp. 95-98.

[120] Rpt of Opns, 2nd Bn, 5th Mar, 2-16 Jun (Records 7).

[121] Memo rpt to CG of inspection of 1st Bn, 5th Mar, 19 Jun (Records 7). These mortars, however, were used by the 23rd Infantry in its assault in Vaux. See memo, CO 23rd Inf for G-2 GHQ AEF, 2 Jul (2nd Div Box 62).

[122] Jnl O, 20 Jun.

the wood continued but without success.[123] Although no gas attacks against the 2nd Division were reported for 21-22 June, the Report of Operations covering those days said that 80 gassed and wounded were evacuated on the 21st, and 78 gassed and wounded were evacuated on the 22nd, including 5 gas cases from the 7th Infantry.

Attrition in the German Forces

If, as a German interrogation report said, "Marine Regiments of the 2nd Division were unable /to capture the remaining portion of Belleau Wood_7 due to the frequently admitted high casualties they had suffered,"[124] the enemy units now opposite the 2nd Division began to report for the first time that they too were suffering from depleted ranks (Map No. 6).

Always reluctant to admit to high battle casualties, and still more reluctant to record gas cases, the Germans had nevertheless been hurt at Chateau Thierry. The high incidence of evacuations from their lines was first attributed to a mysterious gas poisoning of their troops. From the "symptoms of the disease," a German report of 6 June had said, " the suspicion prevails that troops have been poisoned by the blue cross gas which was fired into Chateau-Thierry. The symptoms were described as irritation of the mucous membrane of mouth and throat cavity, difficulty of breathing, "stitches" in the chest, stomach trouble, diarrhea (occasionally bloody), pains in joints, headaches and dizziness."[125] On the 13th it was reported that 6 officers and over 100

---

[123] Jnl O, 22 Jun.

[124] Inter Rpt, 21 Jun (Item 166, 4th Annex, War Diaries 2).

[125] Rpt, CO 3rd Bn, 442nd Inf, 231st Div (Item 216, doc 73, War Diaries 4). Total casualties of this div from 1 Apr-30 Jun were later reported as 313 killed, 1609 wounded, 1786 sick, 147 missing. No gas casualties were reported (Rpt of 231st Div Surgeon, doc 71, War Diaries 4).

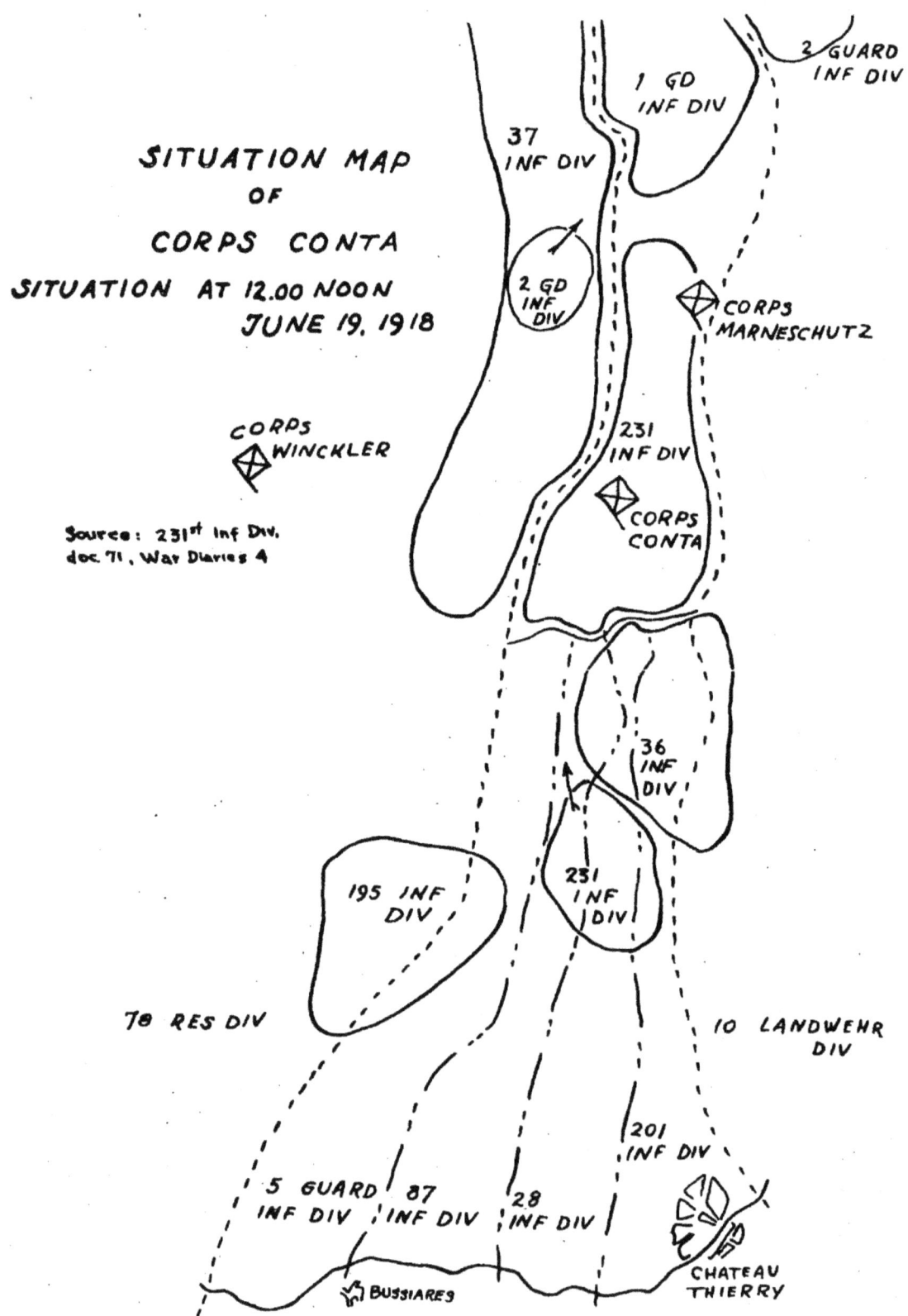

men of the 460th Infantry had fallen sick on 11 and 12 June, seemingly from aftereffects of gas received on 9 June. Combat power of the regiment, as a result, had been reduced "to the lowest."[126]

As General Naulin requested the new French yperite for the 2nd Division on 15 June, it had already been fired by other French artillery units facing the 7th Army, as an Army order of the 15th indicates: "The French are, as a new development, using a gas which is somewhat stronger and has an appreciable more persistent effect than that hitherto used....The gas is hardly noticeable at the beginning of a bombardment; the troops will therefore easily be surprised and...must...be warned to count on gas in every artillery bombardment."[127] Gas protection and gas discipline, the Army order went on, must henceforth assume the highest importance. A brigade order on the same date repeated the warning: "I am again calling attention to the fact that lately the enemy has been using a new type of gas....It is impossible now to remain in gassed areas for extended periods without the gas mask as was the practice heretofore without risking one's life."[128]

---

[126]
 460 Inf (237th Div) to 244th Inf Brig (Item 198, doc 82, War Diaries 4). Ernst Otto, p. 27, reports the combat strength of the 237th Div (minus machine gun and mortar crews) as follows:

460th Inf	21 officers	575 men
461st Inf	12 officers	429 men
462nd Inf	14 officers	478 men

That day 58 NCOs and 150 men were taken from the divisional trains and put in the line.

[127]
 Item 179, 179th Inf Brig, War Diaries 3.

[128]
 55th Inf Brig (Item 178, 40th Fus Regt, War Diaries 2).

Beginning on 19 June, gas and gas sickness reports began to accumulate. The greatest number of casualties were, of course, among the elements of the 28th Division which had for so long been fighting for the Bois de Belleau. As a 40th Fusilier battalion commander said: "All men are over-exhausted as a result of the long periods they have been in the lines and greatly demoralized due to the recent combats at the village of Bouresches and the Bois de Belleau Cases of men gassed increase daily."[129] Since the 16th, said the 40th Fusiliers, almost a hundred in one battalion had fallen sick of the grippe-like poison illness and more were succumbing, "explained by the low resistance powers of the men, who were exhausted by the offensive and above all, by the recent fatiguing position warfare, as well as by the effect of enemy combat gasses."[130] Another 28th Division unit, the 110th Grenadiers, reported that between 13-22 June it had evacuated 127 men wounded and 47 gas cases.[131]

As the first elements of its relief appeared, the German 26th, once a crack outfit reported: "Due to continuous shelling...the nerve strength of the troops steadily depleted....In my opinion I despair whether the division in its present condition is capable of repelling a strong hostile attack." It had lost most of its best officers and NCOs and was short its normal strength

---

[129] 3rd Bn to 40th Fus, 19 Jun (Item 216, 40th Fus, War Diaries 2).

[130] War Diary of 1st Bn, 40th Fus, 20 Jun (War Diaries 3).

[131] Med rpt, Regtl Surg, 110th Gren (Item 1, 55th Inf Brig, War Diaries 2).

by 202 officers, 2,938 men, and 300 (92%) horses.[132] A week later, with its relief cancelled and most of its elements back in the line, the 28th reported: "The severe losses and the many cases of sickness of the past few weeks have further diminished the combat value of the Division." Replacements were meager, for it was still short 194 officers, 2249 men, and 280 horses, and was badly in need of four weeks' rest.[133] A report on the combat effectiveness of the 28th on 4 July declared: "Casualties since 27 May amount to more than 3,000 men." It was still short 207 officers, and now required no less than six weeks for rest and reorganization.[134] The 28th Division had been badly mauled by the 2nd American, but it could not be permitted to leave the line.

On 21 June, Corps Conta was relieved as a command unit and Corps Schoeler (VIIth Army Corps) assumed direction of its forces, comprising the 5th Guard, the 87th and 201st Infantry Divisions, with the newly arrived 4th Ersatz Division and the battered 28th in temporary reserve. Corps Schoeler explained why Corps Conta had failed in its mission to reach its defensive objectives:

---

[132] Combat Value of the Divisions, 28th Div, 20 Jun (Item 236, 4th Annex, War Diaries 2). In addition to gaskranke, there undoubtedly was an epidemic of grippe in the German Armies in the summer of 1918. General Walter Reinhardt, CofS, 7th Army, later said that "on 7 July, each and every division of the entire German Seventh Army counted not less than from 300 to 2000 men stricken with grippe in hospitals." (As They Saw Us, ed. G. S. Viereck, NY: Doubleday, Doran, 1929, pp. 98-99).

[133] Ibid., 27 Jun (Item 163, 5th Annex, War Diaries 2).

[134] Ibid., 4 Jul (Item 222, 6th Annex, War Diaries 2).

"The high casualties of the last battles appear in part to be due to the fact that our infantry continues to mass too thickly at the front and has not sufficient distribution in depth....The important thing is economization of our forces."[135] That same day, 29 June, Corps Schoeler issued its new plan of Defense in depth.[136] It was to prove timely.

The Gas Attack of June 23-24 and the Capture of Belleau Wood

Returning now to the battle-weary 2nd Division side of the line, Intelligence reported late in the month that the German order of battle from Torcy to Vaux comprised the 5th Guard Division, the 87th Division, and the 201st Division, the 402nd Regiment of the latter opposite Vaux, its 401st Regiment opposite Hill 204, and its 403rd Regiment at Chateau Thierry, just outside the 2nd Division sector.[137] The 28th was then on its way back to the slot between the 87th and 201st.

Almost continuously on 22-23 June, German troops were seen moving in large forces north and northeast of Belleau and infiltrating into the wood from the Belleau-Bouresches road. (A German deserter to the French lines on the right said on 25 June that a large-scale assault with a shock division had been planned for that day but was called off.)[138] To break up these

---

[135]
    Corps Hq to Div Comds, 5th Guard, 87th Inf, 28th Inf, 201st Inf, 4th Ersatz Divs, 29 Jun (Item 218, 6th Annex, War Diaries 2).

[136]
    Hq 8th Army Corps, 29 Jun (Items 1-2, 362nd Inf, 4th Er Div, War Diaries 3).

[137]
    SOI 77, 25-26 Jun.

[138]
    FM fr 2nd Bureau, 10th CAC, 3 p.m., 25 Jun.

forces and prepare for another attack, 2nd Division artillery put down a steady fire on the top of the wood and the enemy's back area. With this preparation, the 3rd Battalion, 5th Marines launched a strong attack against the northern part of Belleau Wood at 7:00 p.m. on the 23rd. The attack was indecisive. As the battalion commander said: "The enemy seems to have unlimited alternate gun positions and many guns. Each gun position covered by others. I know of no other way of attacking these positions with chance of success than the one attempted (i.e., rushing the nests by combat groups) and am of the opinion that infantry alone cannot dislodge the enemy guns."[139]

Again, the retaliation for the attack was swift. Just before midnight on 23 June, German 77 and 105mm batteries began to pour gas and HE into the southern part of the Bois de Belleau and around Lucy. In the hour after midnight, Bourbelin, just east of the Bois des Clerembauts, on the 9th Infantry front, was hit with 40 77mm yperite shells, and 600 105mm yperite shells fell in the Bois itself, forcing evacuation of the troops there. Between 3:00 and 4:00 a.m., almost 1,000 88mm yperite shells fell among 23rd Infantry and 5th MG Battalion troops at La Cense Ferme, west of Clerembauts.[140] A German report confirmed the gas bombardment: "Destructive fire on Lucy le

---

[139] FM CO 3rd Bn, 5th Mar to CO 5th Mar, 24 Jun (Records 7).

[140] SOI 75, 23-24 Jun; Rpt Opns, 24 Jun; Rpt on Gas Attack, ser. 18, reports 3000 77mm, 105mm, and 155mm mustard shells in the initial bombardment around midnight against the 5th Marine, 9th and 23rd Infantry sectors, causing 414 casualties. To this Spencer (pp. 128, 133-135) adds 1800-2000 mustard shells in the midnight bombardment and during the hour's follow-up fire at 4:00 a.m., causing 185 gas casualties in the 23rd Inf, 43 in the 5th MG Bn, and 154 in the 9th Inf. This apparent duplication of reports appears again on p. 136 when he reports another 3000 mustard gas rounds at midnight, 25 June, resulting in 350 casualties in the 9th and 23rd Inf.

Hanslian (pp. 102-104) quotes the arty order for the gas shoots and reports a total of 4100 yellow cross shells in the atk on the morning of the 24th.

Bocage. From 12:30 a.m. poison gas shelling with yellow cross shells on the woods of Clerembauts, Triangle, le Thiolet, la Cense, and Vivray Farm. This was followed by systematic gassing."[141] The systematic follow-up gassing continued until well over 4,000 mustard gas shells had been fired by the light and heavy artillery of the 28th Division.

The seriousness of the gas bombardment was not at first recognized. At 11:30 a.m. on the 24th, a company commander of the 23rd Infantry said of his gas cases: "Casualties were...men...observed without masks just after the second gas attack this morning; they are therefore marked not in line of duty."[142] Not until a report of at least a hundred gas cases was made on the afternoon of the 24th was the serious nature of the attack known. At 7:40 p.m. that evening, 162 cases had been reported and Col. Malone sent the following message to Brig. Gen. Lewis at Domptin:

Troops were moved to avoid the effects of gas and masks were worn in some cases for 8 hours and on the average for about 4 hours. Due to the shortage of officers with the troops masks were in some cases prematurely removed especially by the troops recently arrived. Mustard only appeared to have been used. The forward line is now lightly held and the troops are as much disposed as safety will permit. Urgently request replacements.[143]

A message from a machine gun company of the 23rd Infantry said: "After the gas attacks last night and this morning I have not enough men to man my guns and hold the positions."[144]

---

[141] Daily rpt, 23/24 Jun, 28th Div (Item 26, 4th Annex, War Diaries 1).

[142] FM E-2 to CO 23rd Inf (23rd Inf, Records, 5).

[143] FM CO 23rd Inf to CG 3rd Brig.

[144] Daily Rec of Events, CO MG Co 23rd Inf to CO 23rd Inf & Co 5th MG Bn, 24 Jun (Records 7).

The Report of Operations on the 24th listed 104 wounded and gassed from the 9th and 23rd Infantry and 13 from the 7th Infantry. The Journal of Operations later that day corrected the figures to 152 gas casualties in the 9th Infantry, 162 in the 23rd, and 25 in the 5th MG Battalion. The 5th MG Gas Officer subsequently reported 1 officer and 42 men gassed as a result of taking their masks off after four hours, then sleeping in the gassed area.

On the 25th, the Journal of Operations counted 68 wounded and 417 gassed in the 24-hour period ending 6:00 a.m. on the 25th. All gas cases had been removed to the dressing station at Bezu le Guery, five kilometers back of the front line, and then evacuated to the Division Gas Hospital at Luzancy, eight kilometers beyond Bezu.

The Medical Director of the Gas Service, reporting on the attack, said that many of the casualties had resulted from individual carelessness and poor company gas discipline. There was some extenuation, perhaps, in the fact that all the troops were tired after three weeks of combat. A particular hazard, in many of the cases, he said, was the poor protection provided by company dugouts, which in some instances had been little more than gas traps.[145] Another report said the discipline of replacements had been poor for they had remained in the gassed area, showing ignorance of the persistency of mustard. But most cases had resulted when after three hours gas masks had been removed too soon.[146]

---

[145] Lt Col H. L. Gilchrist to C Gas Serv, 1 Jul, Rpt on Second Serious Gas Attack in 2nd Div (GAF-2S).

[146] Rpt on Gas Attack, ser. 18, 9th Inf, 24 Jun (GAF-2A).

The 2nd Division would have been interested in a Corps Schoeler order at that time which urged "economy of blue and green cross ammunition; the use of yellow cross only for defense against enemy attacks is left to the commander's discretion."[147] On the day following the gas strike, enemy troop movement continued and his harassing fire increased on the back areas, but gas shell amounted only to 40 rounds on Lucy le Bocage, possibly in answer to retaliatory gassing by 2nd Division artillery on the early morning of the 25th. German reports of this gassing said: Bois de Borne Agron severely gassed today. Troops had to wear gas masks from 3:15-4:30 a.m. Gas white as mist; apparently chlorine gas. Gas without effect."[148]

Late in the afternoon of the 25th, after an artillery preparation of almost 14 hours on an enemy strongpoint southeast of Torcy and on the top of the Bois de Belleau, the 3rd Battalion, 5th Marines returned to the attack on the wood. In the fight that followed, the Bois was cleared at last, with the capture of 7 German officers, 302 men, and 19 machine guns. It was this final desperate assault on the Bois de Belleau that shattered German hopes of regaining it and moving southward again. Their two counterattacks on the night of 25-26 June, preceded by intense bombardments of the wood with HE, were repulsed, and on the 26th the Marines continued to advance in the area between Torcy and the top of the Bois, pushing the line forward 550 yards and improving

---

[147] In War Diary, 28th Div, 22 Jun (War Diaries 2).

[148] SOI 76, 24-25 Jun; "400 rounds of #17 (?) Mustard gas upon an active enemy battery" (2nd Ind, CO 12th FA to CO 2nd FA Brig, 29 Jan 19 /WD Hist Box 300, S3.6.7).
Combat Rpt, 2nd Bn, 110th Gren (War Diaries 3); Evening Rpt, 55th Inf Brig, 25 Jun (Item 123, 55th Inf Brig, War Diaries 1).

the position, with little opposition (see Map No. 7). The Marine casualties in this decisive action were reported as 160 men.[149]

After light gassing by the enemy of the Bois de Belleau earlier on the night of the 26th, between 8:30 and 11:30 p.m. over 800 mustard-filled 77s fell on the Ru Gobert, north of Maison Blanche. Between 10:20 and 11:10 p.m., the area of Paris Ferme was also bombarded with gas, in an effort to neutralize the batteries there. Although a Marine battalion was forced to march through 600 yards of recently mustardized terrain, the troops, it was reported, wore their masks and escaped casualties. Other unidentified troops in the area did not, for casualties that day were recorded as 42 wounded and 12 gassed.[150]

Up to 1 July, the 2nd Division had advanced its front at some points approximately two kilometers and had taken more than 2,000 prisoners and more than 90 machine guns, minenwerfers, and automatic rifles.[151] But it had been paid for.

The Taking of Vaux

With the final capture of the Bois de Belleau on 25 June, plans long urged by the French Higher Command were set in motion. The 2nd Division was to capture Vaux as soon as possible, while the 153rd French Infantry on the

---

[149]
SOI 77, 78, 25-27 Jun; Jnl O, 25-26 Jun; FM fr Div Surg, 9 a.m., 26 Jun.

[150]
SOI 78, 26-27 Jun; Rpt of Gas Attack, ser. 19, 29 Jun; Jnl O, 27 Jun. Hanslian, pp. 105-106, reports 1000 yellow cross rounds fired by 87th Div arty, but omits casualties, as does Spencer, I. 138.

[151]
Rpt, Opns of 2nd FA Brig (Records 9).

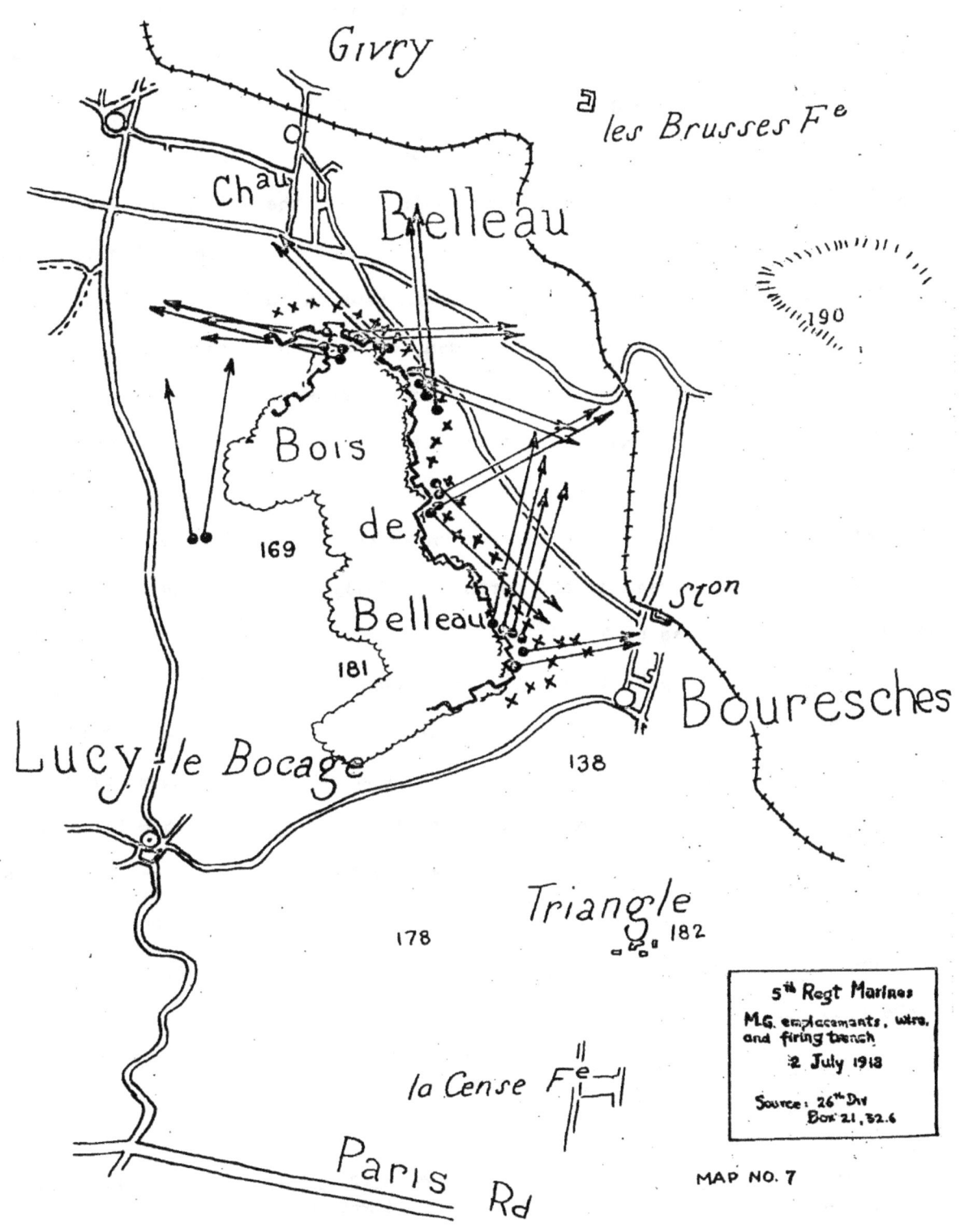

right of the division was to attack Hill 204 and Chateau Thierry itself.

In preparation for the assault on Vaux, scheduled for 1 July, ambush and reconnaissance patrols went out from all units of the 2nd Division, and destructive and harassing fires from the batteries were stepped up. An Information Bulletin issued on 29 June described in detail the village of Vaux and its 82 houses built of flint stone. A battalion of the <u>402nd Regiment</u>, <u>201st Division</u> was said to occupy the area around Vaux, with two battalions in reserve, while a single company of 137 men, of which 90 were combat troops, occupied the village itself. Both roads into Vaux were said to be held with a complex of tank traps and strong barricades, and nine machine gun sites had been located in and on the perimeter of Vaux. Elements of trenches and numbers of machine gun and rifle pits were known to be along the road east of Vaux, and the wooded areas to the north were fully fortified and manned, with at least five batteries of 77s.[152]

As 2nd Division patrol activity was stepped up on 29-30 June, enemy artillery fire greatly increased and was answered with harassing and counter-battery fire. The attack troops of the 23rd and 9th Infantry moved into position on the night of 30 June and waited in concealment, "but without adequate protection, for 15 hours under a heavy bombardment before beginning the attack. In spite of these difficulties, the attack moved with mechanical perfection, with no fault of liaison, and was carried to its conclusion with complete success."[153]

---

[152] Info Bul preceding SOI 80.

[153] SOI 81, 29-30 Jun; memo CO 23rd Inf for G-2 GHQ AEF, 2 Jul, sub: Opns of 23rd Inf, Jul 1, 1918 (2nd Div Box 62, 33.6 Rpt of Opns).

At 5:00 p.m. on 30 June, the artillery preparation for the attack on Vaux began with the bombardment of Hill 204 and the village itself. At the same hour on 1 July the enemy counter-offensive preparation answered, with a torrent of fire on the vicinity of Monneaux and Hill 204. Soon after, the area south of the Bois de Belleau and then the front lines in the vicinity of Bouresches and the Bois des Clerembauts were swept with shell. It was by far the greatest concentration of fire of the campaign, as an estimated 21,500 shells from German 77s, 105s, and 150s poured into the area before Vaux. In the counter-offensive preparation, the enemy "gassed all wooded areas near the front," including 500 rounds of mustard gas and phosgene in and around Vaux.[154] Over 33,000 rounds of HE and gas fell on that corner alone of the 2nd Division sector.

After the divisional artillery preparation of 500 rounds per hour for more than twelve hours, including a three-hour gas shelling from four batteries of the 15th F.A. on the woods northeast of Vaux,[155] at 6:00 p.m. on 1 July a battalion each from the 23rd and 9th Infantry attacked the line Vaux-Bois de la Roche. Enemy forces emerging from the houses in the utterly demolished village put up little defense before fleeing into the nearby Bois des Rochets. The close fighting was of short duration, and consolidation of the position began an hour and a half after the assault. Six German officers and 434 men,

---

[154] SOI 82, 83, 30 Jun-2 Jul.

[155] Rpt, Opns of 2nd FA Brig. A postwar rpt by the 15th FA said it fired 6000 75mm yperite shells between 1:00-5:00 p.m. on 1 Jul (Ind on ltr OC Arty to CG 2nd FA Brig, 13 Jan 19, sub: Info requested by CWS AEF. WD Hist Box 300, 33.6).
Noon rpt, 2 Jul, 201st Div shows 19 gas casualties on 1-2 Jul in 402nd Inf (Item 254, 28th Div, 6th Annex, War Diaries 2).

most of them routed from the cellars of the leveled houses, were taken prisoner, along with six heavy and eighteen light machine guns.[156] In contrast, the French attack on Hill 204, to the right, failed.

"Our losses were very light" in the Vaux action, said division reports, with one officer and 45 men killed, 6 officers and 264 men wounded, and one officer and 11 men missing.[157] There was no mention of gas casualties. A heavy machine gun barrage and artillery fire, including approximately 500 phosgene shells in the ravine from Vaux to Monneaux, preceded an enemy counterattack on Vaux at 4:15 a.m. on 2 July, but both the barrage and attack were reported ineffectual by the division, the Germans losing an additional officer and 140 men as prisoners.[158] Nevertheless, casualties for the 24-hour period ending 6:00 a.m. on 2 July reported as 121 men wounded, 37 men gassed, and 2 officers wounded and gassed.[159]

Over in the Marine sector during this counterattack, a German report said, there was "brisk rifle and machine gun fire on our posts /‾at 4:15 a.m._/ Patrols noticed enemy activity at the north edge of Belleau Wood,

---

[156] Jnl O, 1 Jul.

[157] SOI 83, 1-2 Jul; Rpt of Opns, 2 Jul.

[158] The German rpt on this gassing in support of the 201st Div said: "From 3:00 a.m. on blue cross drenching floating-gas bombardments on Marette Wood. At dawn barrage and destructive fire waves. Today harassing fire on the la Marette, Clerembauts, and la Croisette Woods." (Daily Rpt for 1/2 Jul, 28th Div, Item 281, 6th Annex, War Diaries 2). Hanslian, p. 107, reports 3350 blue cross shells fired by the 28th and 201st Divs into the Bois de la Marette and Monneaux valley beginning 2:30 a.m., 2 July, and 1130 yellow cross and 1200 blue and green cross rounds into those areas at noon 4 Jul -- but cannot justify Spencer's data, pp. 139-143, showing 8000 gas shells on 1,2,3 July, producing 177 casualties. 2nd Div records agree with neither.

[159] SOI 84, 2-3 Jul.

fallen trees and other obstacles placed opposite the right wing of our sector. Our artillery laid harassing fire all night on Belleau Wood and rear areas. Enemy artillery shelled our batteries with gas and harassing fire (see Map No. 6)."[160]

"Towards 10:00 p.m." on 2 July a French artillery unit seems to have fired "about 30 gas shells medium caliber on the ravine south of Bonne."[161] Shortly after 11:00 p.m., the enemy artillery retaliated for Vaux and Bonne with almost 5,000 mixed HE and gas shells along the new 2nd Division front, other gas on the Bois de la Marette and Clerembauts, and on other sensitive points as far west as La Cense Ferme and Triangle Ferme. The Germans reported: "From 12:00 to 2:00 a.m. yellow cross drenching bombardments were carried out on Bois des Clerembauts, Thiolet, and the adjoining farms."[162]

With the first gas shells, Malone of the 23rd Infantry called his companies: "Keep masks on all night if necessary, dispose your troops to avoid results. Be careful of repetition of attack later in the morning. Get disinfecting squads on the job at day break (FM to E-1, 11:45 p.m., 2 Jul, Records 5)." All through the night of 2-3 July, the German batteries continued their intense fire, throwing almost 12,000 rounds of HE, in addition to the gas, into the divisional sector, with the heaviest fire along the new front. At 6:00 a.m., 3 July, 294 men were reported wounded.[163]

---

[160] 87th Div WD, 2 Jul (87th Div-Sub Units-WD&A, 14 Jun-30 Jul, p. 128 /German Files Box 204_/).

[161] Tele comm, 87th Inf Div to 28th Div (Item 269, 6th Annex, War Diaries 2).

[162] SOI 84, 2-3 Jul; Morning Rpt, 28th Div, 3 Jul (Item 271, 6th Annex). Hanslian, pp. 109-110, reports a gas bombardment of 4150 yellow cross shells by 28th Div arty beginning at midnight, 2-3 Jul, and cites the arty order for this shelling of Clerembauts and le Thiolet.

[163] Jnl O, 2-3 Jul. Spencer, I. 141, reporting 2500 mustard gas shells from 11:00 p.m.-1:00 a.m., 2-3 Jul, says 41 men were gassed.

On the morning of 3 July, enemy artillery fire slackened, only to resume later in the day. Beginning at 11:45 that night all wooded areas on the extreme right of the line were gassed, with more than 1,500 rounds of yperite and phosgene 77s and 105s on the Bois de la Marette, 20 rounds of yperite on the Bois de la Roche, 30 rounds of yperite on the Bois des Clerembauts, and 200 mixed HE, shrapnel, and yperite on Bourbelin. Casualties reported for the period ending 6:00 a.m. on 4 July were 2 officers and 30 men wounded, 86 men gassed.[164]

On 4 July, the long-awaited relief of the 2nd Division commenced, as elements of the 52nd Brigade, 26th Division, came in to replace the shattered 4th Brigade. Further relief was postponed the next day when information was received that a large-scale German attack was about to be made somewhere in the area between Reims and Chateau Thierry.[165] That same day, the 5th, 2nd Division Intelligence reported a new German order of battle opposite the division. The 4th Ersatz Division was now between Bussiares and Belleau, relieving a part of the 87th, the 87th was between Belleau and Bouresches, the 28th between Bouresches and Vaux, and the 201st encircling Vaux.[166] (This seems partially contradicted by Map No. 8).

---

[164] SOI 85, 3-4 Jul; Jnl O, 4 Jul.

[165] Jnl O, 4 Jul; War Diary, 5 Jul.

[166] SOI 86, 4-5 Jul.

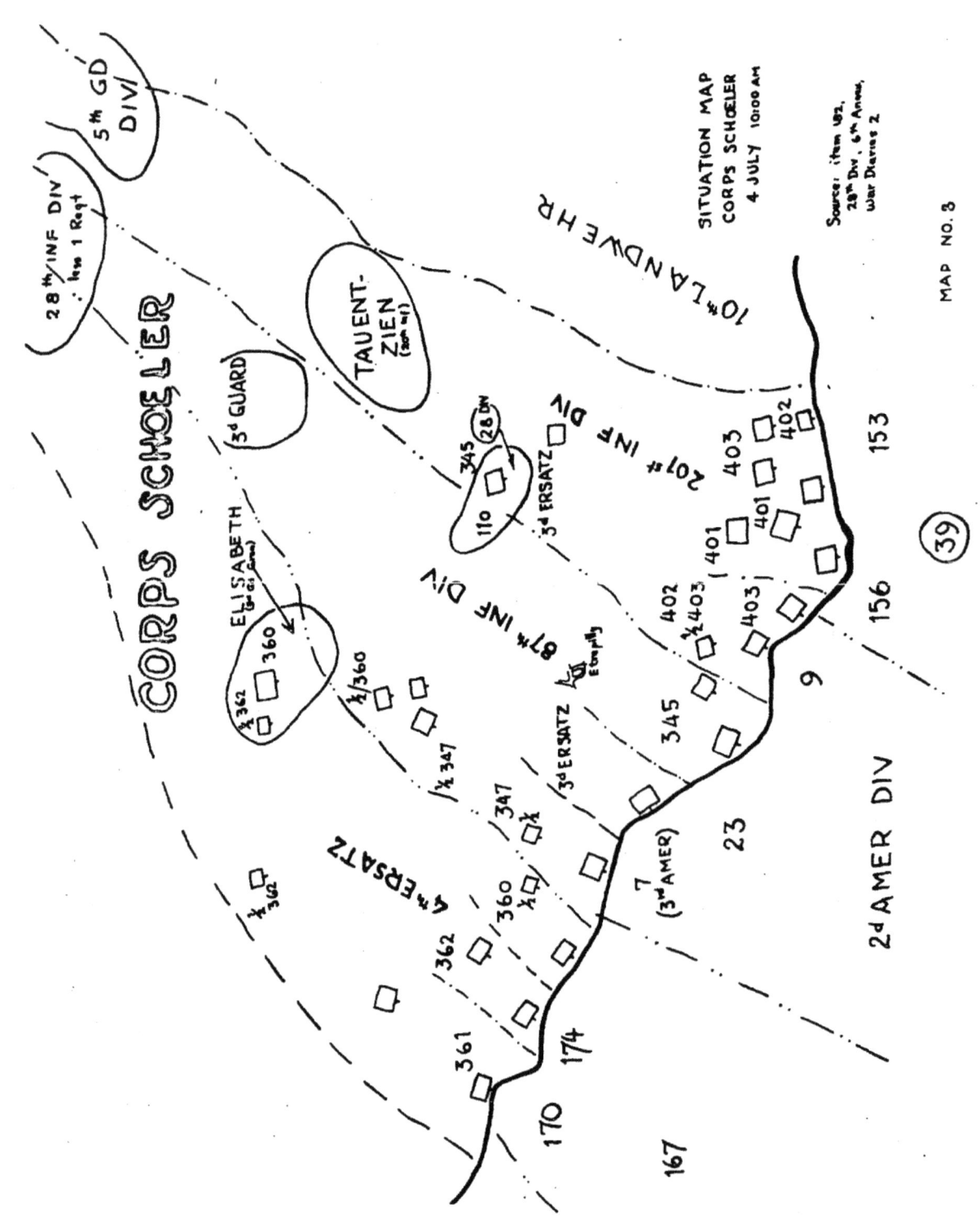

Artillery fire returned to normal over the week that followed as the 2nd Division showed no disposition to be dislodged from Vaux, but gas shells continued to fall on the wooded areas in the division sector, 350 yperite-filled 77s and 105s hitting the Bois de la Marette between 11:45 and 3:00 a.m. on the night of 4-5 July, and almost 200 HE gas shells falling just east of Tuilerie de Triangle. Casualties at 6:00 a.m. on the 5th were reported as 1 officer and 31 men wounded, 119 gassed.[167] On 5 July, preceded by a rear area bombardment and a surprise gas attack on German forces at le Buisson, the French returned to the assault on Hill 204, which they had failed to take the day Vaux was captured. Again they were repulsed.[168]

In the reprisal shelling of the sector during the day of the 5th, HE and gas accounted for 2 officers gassed and wounded, 12 men wounded, and 27 men gassed.[169] Further reprisal for the French gas came between 7:30 p.m. and midnight on 6 July when Monneaux and the vicinity of Bourbelin were bombarded with over 400 blue cross shells, and 75 gas shells hit the Bois de la Marette. The next morning 38 men were reported wounded and 2 officers and 19 men gassed.[170] On the night of 7 July, approximately 650 gas shells, mixed with HE and shrapnel, were fired into the Bois de la Marette, with

---

[167] SOI 86, 4-5 Jul; Jnl O, 5 Jul. Spencer, I, 143, reports 88 casualties as a result of mustard gas shelling on the early morning of the 5th.

[168] War Diary of 201st Inf Div, 6 Jul (War Diaries 3).

[169] Jnl O, 6 Jul. Cf. Tel message, Corps Schoeler to 28th Div, 11:50 p.m., 6 Jul (Item 145-46, 6th Annex, War Diaries 2): "Bois de la Roche NW of Vaux and the village of Vaux were subjected to harassing fire and blue cross gas bombardments."

[170] SOI 88, 6-7 Jul; Jnl O, 7 Jul; Div Order, 201st Inf Div, 5 Jul (War Diaries 3).

scattered gas shells falling in the Bois de Belleau. Casualties were reported the next morning to be 18 wounded, one officer and 7 men gassed.[171]

The relief of the 2nd Division was resumed on 7 July as rumors of the new German assault failed to materialize. On the night of 8-9 July, the last elements of the division cleared the line, reassembling between Montreuil-aux-Lions and Bezu le Guery, ten kilometers back of the front. At the same time division headquarters was moved from Genevrois Farm down to Champigny.[172]

Although the 2nd Division had gained no more than a kilometer or two of terrain in its month of fighting, it had done more than its share to brake the Third German Drive, and it had forced the enemy from the offensive to the defensive, from open warfare to trench warfare, just when he thought he had achieved maneuverability again.

---

[171] SOI 89, 7-8 Jul; Jnl O, 8 Jul.

[172] Jnl O, 9 Jul.

ANALYSIS

German Artillery Fire

Beginning on 5-6 June, the Summaries of Intelligence give, with a few exceptions, the estimated number of enemy HE shells (all calibers) falling on the left of the divisional sector, the estimated number falling on the right of the sector; and, only incidentally and with many lapses, the estimated total of gas shells falling in the entire sector.

As of 7-8 July, the number of recorded HE shell falling in the left sector since 5 June totals 65,675, and on the right, 120,085. The grand total of HE shell fired at the 2nd Division therefore comes to 185,760. The grand total or recorded gas shell fired at the Division is reported as 13,540 or 6% of the total artillery shell.[173]

The gas shell figure must be considered minimal in view of omissions in divisional data. Despite a German Corps Order of 22 June urging "economy of blue and green cross ammunition; the use of yellow cross only for defense..." (narrative, p. 54), the 2nd Division was aware of no economy. At the beginning of the Third German Drive on 27 May (the Aisne offensive), the Germans seem to have had large supplies of gas shell, for a captured order of the 7th Army dated 8 May says that in counterbattery and long range bombardment, the ratio of shell was to be blue cross 70%, green cross 10%, HE 20%. In the bombardment of enemy positions, the ratio in creeping

---

[173] These are hasty calculations. The figures given in German accounts of gas shelling and cited in the narrative have not been collated with the SOI figures. No effort has been made to distinguish between kinds of gas, although the weight of yellow cross was by far the greatest.

barrages would be blue cross 30%, green cross 10%, HE 60%, and in box barrages the ratio would be blue cross 60%, green cross 10%, HE 30%.[174] Unaccountably, there is no mention in this order of yellow cross gas.

The French and Americans west of Chateau Thierry at no time experienced anything like the weights of gas fired in earlier bombardments against the Allies. In three successive nights, 11-14 March 1918, the British at Cambrai, for example, were overwhelmed by almost 150,000 yellow cross shells. But the amount of gas in the American sector seemed impressive to the forces there. In a report, "Enemy Gas Operations for the Month of June 1918," Capt. B. C. Goss, Eng., CGO 1st Army Corps, 9 July, he said:

> The month of June has shown considerable increase in the use of chemical shell by the enemy, it being estimated that approximately 50,000 gas shells were fired on the sectors held by the First Corps units. No projector attacks were made, and no chemical grenades were reported. Yellow cross 1 shells, containing dichlorethylarsine and dichlormethyl ether were used for the first time on our troops on June 3rd in the Bois de Belleau. The only other new feature of interest was the increased use of larger caliber and longer range projectiles containing gas, i.e., considerable numbers of 150 and 210mm shells filled with Yellow cross liquid and a few containing phenyl carbylamine chloride. The chemicals used were chiefly yellow cross (dichlorethylsulphide), blue cross (diphenylchlorarsine) and green cross 1 (diphosgene and chlorpicrin).[175]

---

[174] Quoted in Victor Lefebure, Riddle of the Rhine (London, 1921), p. 73; "There is evidence that the supply of gas shells for Corps Conta artillery was maintained during the advance from the Chemin des Dames." The 28th Div Order 1321, issued on 5 June, for the planned attack on the 7th (Item 221-22, 1st Annex, War Diaries 2), said that all artillery from X to X plus 10 would engage hostile batteries and battle positions with blue cross; X plus 10 to X plus 30 all guns would prepare for the assault with HE, with blue cross added for the first ten minutes to force the enemy into masks; and from X plus 30 to X plus 60 all light and heavy howitzers would provide a rolling barrage of HE in rounds of 300 meters at ten-minute intervals. Interdictory fire with yellow cross was apparently not considered for this attack.

[175] WD Hist-CWS-Box 300 (33.6) and GAF (fol 1st C, 1st A). The gas atk of 3 June rptd in the letter does not agree with earlier reports (see narrative, p. 22).

Since the U. S. divisions of the First Corps in combat that month included the 1st, 2nd, 26th, and 42nd Divisions, and the estimated number of gas shells fired at them, according to this report, was 50,000, perhaps the above total of 13,540 shells in the 2nd Division sector is not grossly inaccurate.

One statistic for the period between 4 June and 8 July seems incontrovertible: in those 35 days there were only four days free of gas.[176] The daily necessity for wearing the gas mask, sometimes for prolonged periods at a time, unquestionably contributed to the progressive exhaustion of the 2nd Division.

The Casualties of the 2nd Division

The "Record of Casualties" compiled by the 2nd Division Statistical Section,[177] giving detailed figures for the seven campaigns of the division, indicates that over 78% of the total gas casualties suffered during the war occurred in the single month near Chateau Thierry and more than 32% of the total casualties that month were caused by gas:

---

[176] SOI, 5 Jun-8 Jul; ltr, Capt Charles H. Gorrill, Eng., CGO 3rd AC to CGO 3rd A, 8 Feb 19, sub: Rpt on Gas Attacks (GAF-2S and WD Hist-CWS-Box 300 33.6).

[177] Records 6. Much of the data appears also in ltr CG 2nd Div to ACS G-3 GHQ AEF, 30 Dec 18, sub: Opns info re 2nd Div (2nd Div Box 5, 11.4, and Box 29, 33.6).

	Total casualties		Gas casualties	
	Officers	Men	Officers	Men
Verdun	12	826	4	319
Chateau Thierry	217	9560	41	3111
Soissons	154	5780	16	191
St. Mihiel	43	1590	–	23
Champagne	209	4766	12	212
Argonne	97	3202	3	85
Marbach	1	46	–	–
	733	23699 *	76	3942

*These total casualties may be compared with the figures in the Army Almanac (1950), p. 666, showing 11,746 Army and 11,348 Marine KIA and WIA, for a total of 23,094. Leonard P. Ayres, The War with Germany: A Statistical Summary (GPO, 1919), shows KIA 4419, WIA 20,657, for a total of 25,076. Shipley Thomas, History of the AEF (New York, 1920), p. 453, shows KIA 4742, WIA 27,872, for a total of 25,989 (sic).

The Statistical Section breakdown of casualties at Chateau Thierry shows:

	Killed		Missing		Severely wounded		Slightly wounded		Gassed		Total	
3rd Brig	17	287	1	107	15	400	12	996	23	1394	68	3184
4th Brig	25	731	1	93	37	890	47	2004	16	1355	126	5073
2nd FA Brig	–	36	–	18	2	51	2	16	–	–	4	121
2nd Eng	6	130	–	54	1	119	7	377	2	273	16	953
4th MG Bn	–	9	–	2	–	7	1	20	–	–	1	38
Others	–	19	–	12	–	16	2	55	–	89	2	191
	48	1212	2	286	55	1483	71	3468	41	3111**	217	9560

**On 11 Jun, the 16th Field Hosp joined the 15th Field Hosp at Luzancy to take care of 2nd Div gassed and sick. From 11 Jun-8 Jul, Luzancy treated 2358 gassed, 22 wounded, 45 shell concussion, 52 injured, 840 sick - a total of 3317. Of these, 500 were returned to duty without further evacuation. (Ltr CG 2nd San Tr to CG 2nd Div, 24 Feb 19, sub: Rpt of Opns, Med Dept, May 31 to July 10, 1918. In Med Dept (2nd Div) Box 3411, fol 13.)

This gas casualty total of 3,152 in the 2nd Division while at Chateau Thierry is challenged by a number of reports. The Monthly Gas Casualty Report, 2nd Division, for month ending 30 June, shows a total of 1,993 gas casualties, to which approximately 300 should be added for 1-8 July.[178] The Monthly Gas Casualty Report, 1st Corps, for month ending 30 June, shows 1,988 gas casualties for the 2nd Division (with 3,135 for the whole Corps).[179] The Division Gas Officer in a letter to the Chief, CWS, 8 February 1919, reported gas casualties at Chateau Thierry as 1691, with total battle casualties in all campaigns amounting to 24,432, of which 3,160 were gas casualties.[180]

This discrepancy between the figures of 3,111, 1,993 plus 300, 1,988 plus 300, and 1,691 for total gas casualties suffered by the 2nd Division at Chateau Thierry cannot at the moment be resolved. Accepting the figures of the Statistical Section, 2nd Division, the gas casualties represent 32% of total casualties. Accepting a median between the two Monthly Gas Casualty Reports (i.e., 2,290), and the total casualties reported by the Statistical Section, the gas casualties represent 23% of the total casualties in the campaign.[181]

---

[178] GAF-2C. Additional 300 based on Jnl O reports for the period.

[179] GAF-fol 1st C, 1st A. Here too is rpt of 9 Jul, CGO 1st AC, Enemy Gas Opns for Month of June 1918, previously cited, which lists 3,144 Corps casualties.

[180] Capt J.S. Craigue, Eng., sub: Circ Ltr No. 89 (GAF-2C and WD Hist-CWS-Box 300). His breakdown of gas casualties at Chateau Thierry is: 3rd Brig, 939; 4th Brig, 551; 2nd FA Brig, 5; 2nd Eng, 62; 4th MG Bn, 86; others, 48.

[181] Cf. ltr Gilchrist Med Dir CWS to C CWS, 18 Aug, sub: Battle and Gas Casualties in the AEF (GAF, 10F7-18a), which reports total battle casualties in AEF between 15-30 June as 12,030 and total gas casualties as 6,218.

Using Statistical Section figures again, we may say that enemy HE artillery fire (estimated in divisional records at 185,760 rounds), together with rifle, machine gun, grenade, and mortar fire, in that month of combat produced 6,625 killed, severely wounded, and slightly wounded, while approximately 13,540 gas shells (no other gas munitions were used) produced 3,152 gas casualties. Comparing the HE artillery shell alone, 29 shells were necessary to achieve each HE casualty in the 2nd Division, whereas only 4.3 artillery gas shells were required to achieve a gas casualty. Even doubling the number of gas shells reveals that 7.2 shells were sufficient to produce a gas casualty.

The much-quoted letter of 25 June 1918 from Col. Paul B. Malone, commander of the 23rd Infantry, is of interest and partially corroborates the foregoing data:

> Enemy artillery fire of all kinds has produced in this regiment a total of about 855 casualties since 1 June. Of these, 334 were produced by gas. The 334 casualties were produced by firing not more than 4,000 gas shells...It would therefore appear, roughly speaking, that the 4,000 gas shells had produced 334 casualties while approximately 116,000 shells of other varieties, machine gun fire, etc., had produced the remaining 521 casualties....(Thus)the gas shell has been approximately nine times as effective as any other form of projectile in producing casualties....The above data is furnished with the view of emphasizing once more the very great importance of securing large quantities of yperite with which to launch a gas offensive while awaiting the time to come when a mobile offensive may be launched.[182]

If gas casualties were not quite that disproportionate in the 2nd Division, they were still alarmingly high, and led to increased numbers of warnings and repeated prescriptions of gas defense principles. As a 1st

---

[182] Ltr to Adj 2nd Div G-1, 25 Jun 18, sub: Use of Gas (GAF-2S, 2nd Div Summaries; also in the 1st Div Box 173, corresp. No. 9946).

Corps Heavy Artillery memo was to say on 15 July:

> The casualties from gas in this sector very greatly outnumber those from wounds....All commanders of units will personally see to the establishment and maintenance of preventive measures....These prescriptions will be carried out rigorously; in addition unit commanders will doubtless find other means of combating this danger peculiarly applicable to their own positions, and it is their duty to put such into effect with reference to higher authority (1st C Box 36, 60.10).

Gas Shell Fired by 2nd Division Artillery

In a postwar report by the 2nd Field Artillery Brigade, it was stated that the 12th F.A. fired no gas shell at Chateau Thierry.[183] The 12th F.A. reported that on 14-15 June, between 11:00 p.m. and 4:00 a.m., it fired 1,700 French No. 5 shells (collognite and opacite, i.e., phosgene and stannic chloride). On July 1, between 1:00-5:00 p.m., it fired 6,000 No. 20 shells (yperite).

On 16 June, at 11:00 p.m., the 17th F.A. (155mm) fired 50 No. 5 shells, on 2 July at 10:00 p.m. it fired 10 No. 5 shells, and on 3 July it fired 20 No. 5 shells, all as "neutralization fire on hostile batteries." "No gas shells were fired," said the 17th F.A. Regimental Gas Officer, "in an American or Allied attack."

This report is considerably at variance, both in numbers and fillings, with 2nd Division reports of the gas reprisal on 15 June (narrative, p. 40). It does not mention the gas shoot on 18 June (pp. 40-41), but it appears to agree with the gas missions of 1-2 July (pp. 57-58). It is in even

---

[183] 3 Inds on ltr OC Arty AEF to CG 2nd FA Brig, 13 Jan 19, sub: Info requested by CWS AEF (WD Hist-CWS-Box 300, 33.6).
At variance with this report is 2nd Ind, McKell, CO 12th FA to CO 2nd FA Brig, 29 Jan 19 (WD Hist Box 300, 33.6, Use of Gas by Arty): "On 25th June, 1918, Battery F, 12th F.A. fired about 400 rounds of #17 /?/ Mustard gas upon an active enemy battery and resulted in silencing it. The enemy battery was never heard from thereafter."
See narrative p. 54.

greater disagreement with German reports of 6-10 June (p. 26), 12 June (p. 30), 13 June (p. 31), 15 June (p. 40), 16-17 June (pp. 42-43, 47-48) and 25 June (p. 54), which describe "2nd Division" gas shelling of their positions.

These German reports indicate that frequent gas attacks were made against them, but if so the missions were fired by the French artillery in the neighboring sector or that attached to the 2nd Division, rather than by the organic artillery. There is some indication (see p. 47) that shortly after General Naulin requested the new yperite for the division, it was used by either the attached or neighboring French artillery. Not until 1 July was any quantity of yperite made available to 2nd Division artillery, when the 15th F.A. reportedly fired 6,000 rounds into the woods north of Vaux.

There is additional evidence of gassing of German terrain by other than the 2nd F.A. Brigade, not included in the narrative account;

Enemy artillery engaged our position especially in the Rochet Wood and in Chateau Thierry, with harassing fire, in part mixed with gas, and shelled our approach roads (1st Morning Rpt to 28th Inf Div, 6 a.m. 14 Jun, item 139, 2nd Annex, War Diaries 2).

From 3:00 to 6:00 a.m. the front line positions were repeatedly shelled with gas shells (Noon Rpt, 28th Arty Comd, 21 Jun, Item 209, 4th Annex, War Diaries 2).

Unfortunately, no French records have as yet been found telling how much gas their artillery units used while in support of the 2nd Division, nor do any 2nd Division records so far examined mention the use of gas by the attached French artillery. French artillery was under VI French Army control and quite independent of either the 2nd F.A. Brigade or the 2nd Division itself.

The situation thus created an irony in our operations: when the French artillery fired gas, the 2nd Division took gas casualties in the retaliation. It was like that other irony of the operation: when the Marines attacked, the Infantry suffered most in the reprisal fire.

The Use of Gas at Belleau Wood

Despite the numbers of gas casualties that the 2nd Division was taking daily, the few expressions so far found of desire or intention to retaliate are those in the Operations Report of the 2nd F.A. Brigade and in General Naulin's letters and orders (pp. 38-39), in the 2nd Division War Diary for the 14th (p. 40), in Grant's letter of the 15th (pp. 44-45), and in Col. Malone's Field Message of the 15th (pp. 36-37).

The anonymous MS history, "The Second Division at Chateau Thierry," has several pencilled comments initialled by Col. Preston Brown, Division Chief of Staff. It may therefore be presumed that he read the MS, at least in part, and agreed with its contents where he did not note an objection. The following has no pencilled comment:

It was decided on the 9th of June to make another forward move on the Bois de Belleau. It may be said in a general way that the real way to deal with a position of this sort was by gas bombardment. The total area of the wood is small; it was isolated from the next supporting enemy position; and however strongly held with rifles and machine guns its resisting power could have been reduced to almost nothing by a mustard preparation of a few hours. But the trouble was that there was no mustard gas available. The Division had been rushed in; its artillery had been gotten up some hours before in the same sort of scramble; and the obtaining of any sort of munitions for the artillery had come about merely through the energy of the command. The Division as a fighting unit was not equipped for dealing with the problem of the Belleau wood. The thing had therefore resolved itself into almost a straight infantry proposition, which it should not have been.[184]

To these observations should be added that of the Marine battalion commander (p. 51) who said of the frustrated attack of 23 June on the Bois: "I know of no other way of attacking these positions with chance of success than the one attempted (i.e., rushing the nests by combat groups) and am of

---

[184] Hist Sec GS AEF, Paris, 1918, p. 37 (2nd Div Box 8, 18.2).

the opinion that infantry alone cannot dislodge the enemy guns." Had the allotment of yperite not arrived at the depot by the 23rd? Or could it, at General Naulin's orders, be used only in reprisal? Yet on 1 July it was used in the assault on Vaux.

It seems clear that to a large extent both our own and enemy HE artillery fire on the Bois de Belleau was nerve-shattering but non-casualty producing, the dense growth and boulder formations dissipating much of the HE effect. German gassing of the wood was restricted for the most part to its edges. But when the southern sector was saturated, the area became wholly untenable. Did the German forces not have mustard gas enough to interdict the whole of the wood and keep it that way while they advanced down its sides? The records so far examined give no clue.

An apparently reliable history of the 2nd Division says that for several days after 13-14 June, the Germans, could they have mustered strength enough, might have occupied the entire Bois, except for the gassed strip on the southern edge, evacuated by the Marines. The wood was fully open to them to the left and rear, with 23rd Infantry machine gunners only along the eastern edge. As it was, the artillerymen on both sides continued their heavy fire, but the opposing infantry forces were by then too spent, either for the Germans to seize their opportunity or for the Americans to have opposed them.[185] Ultimately, it was the artillery that smashed the Germans in

---

[185] O. L. Spaulding and J. W. Wright, The Second Division, AEF, in France, 1917-1919 (Hist Comm, 2nd Div Assn, New York, Hillman Press, 1937), pp. 61-62.

the wood, leading to its capture on 25 June.[186] The Marine commander who said that taking the Bois was no job for the infantry might also have added that it would be a long and costly job for the artillery as well.

The Gas Discipline of the 2nd Division

It is a matter of statistical record that 2nd Division casualties were the highest in the AEF. It was the second American division to go into combat, but in its 137 days of fighting it took almost 5% more casualties than the 1st Division. Both its Marine and Infantry components were, according to German accounts of their actions in the assault, reckless in combat, and, in the eyes of their Gas Officers, careless, to say the least, in the combat zone.

General Order 79, GHQ, AEF, 27 May 1918, called the "attention of all ranks...to the increasing importance of gas warfare," and the stream of bulletins and memoranda from GHQ and the Gas Service to the troop commands were designed to keep them alert to the progress of gas warfare and gas defense.[187] The training and retraining of the 2nd Division in gas defense up to the time it entrucked for Chateau Thierry has already been recounted (pp. 5-8, 14-15). The reactions of the Gas Officers of the Division and Corps to the conduct of the troops under gas attack are also recorded in the narrative (pp. 10-12, 36, 53). Blue and green cross gas seems to have given relatively

---

[186] Ibid., p. 69. General Bundy, in "The Second Division at Chateau Thierry," *Everybody's Magazine*, XL (Mar. 1919), 19, seems to agree with this verdict.

[187] Gas Service Intel Sec, Weekly Summaries of Information, began on 29 Jan 18; Gas Service Intelligence Bulletins first appeared in March 18. See file of these in WD Hist-CWS-Box 298.

little trouble, but to the end of the campaign the 2nd Division could not predict the reactions of its troops to mustard gas. Instructions in defense against mustard seem to have been adequate, yet the unit officers and men continued to forget, in the excitement of battle, the persistency and toxicity of the agent. With time and familiarity, gas casualties seem to have become accepted as, to some degree, unavoidable and inevitable.

The change in attitude from earlier strictures appears in two reports on the mustard attack of 14-15 June. Colonel Preston Brown, Chief of Staff, said on 16 June:

> The gas discipline of the men is excellent, and every man had and used his mask. The casualties were largely due to body burns, caused by clothing saturated with mustard gas. These we consider unavoidable casualties, when it is recognized that the troops occupied wooded and thickly grassed positions which had to be held.
>
> The evacuation of wounded, hospital service, and general efficiency of the medical department has been beyond criticism and has been just as well as it could have been done, in my opinion, in a complicated map problem.
>
> All gassed men were promptly bathed at the dressing stations, their clothing taken away and they were sent wrapped in blankets to the field hospitals.
>
> The approximate number of gas casualties is 900, but it must be borne in mind that the division is under a constant and violent bombardment of gas and high explosive of all calibers, with gas mixed in with shell and shrapnel.[188]

Several days later, Colonel Gilchrist reported to the Chief of Gas Service, AEF:

---

[188] Memo for Col H. L. Gilchrist (Med Dept-2nd Div-Box 3410, fol. 7).

The general gas discipline and morale of the troops during the bombardment was good. From all accounts, proper gas alarms were sounded in ample time for the adjustment of respirators, but in lieu of existing conditions -- a pitch dark night, exploding shells on all sides, heavy underbrush, expected attack from the enemy, and the fact that the troops were worn out from several days of incessant fighting during which time they had little or no rest -- they were in a state of physical depression and in fit condition for the action of poisonous gases. Again, many were scattered throughout the areas asleep on the ground, and during the rush and darkness a few of these men were not awakened in time to apply their respirators.

Some of the men had their respirators knocked off by the explosion of shells, colliding with trees, underbrush, etc. Many were compelled to remove them in order to see, still others removed the facepieces alone, and retained the mouthpieces and noseclip. From a careful study of all conditions connected with this gas attack, it is the opinion that little, if any, criticism can be offered concerning the actions of the officers and men during the attack.[189]

The high casualties following this attack, preventable or not, led 2nd Division headquarters to issue a memorandum on 17 June, "Orders for Gas Defense -- Training and Inspection," which said that all ranks whose duties required them in the danger zone would continue respirator drill. Respirators would be worn at least four hours per week while normal duties were performed. Respirators and gas equipment in the division area were to be inspected twice each week by gas officers and daily in the alert zone by gas NCOs. It emphasized that the only authorized gas masks were the British and American S.B.R.'s. The M2 mask was to be carried only by labor troops stationed five miles or more back of the front; the French Tissot mask was restricted to special troops. The memorandum concluded with standing orders on the action

---

[189] Ltr, Med Dir, Gas Serv, 20 Jun 18, sub: Rpt of Recent Gas Attack on 2nd Div (ibid.).

- 75 -

to be taken by officers and men during and after a gas attack.[190]

Outside the serious attack of 23-24 June, gas casualties in the 2nd Division after 15 June occurred daily, ranging between 7 and 119 per day, until the division was relieved on 8-9 July. They were accepted without comment.

The Strategy at Chateau Thierry

Matthew B. Ridgeway, in his recent memoirs, Soldier (New York: Harper, 1956, pp. 29, 97), has said that World War I was "a conflict which gave to history many prize examples of men's lives being thrown away against objectives which were not worth the cost....a monument, for all time, to the inflexibility of military thinking in that period." The stand of the 2nd Division west of Chateau Thierry was such an example, in that the opponents slugged it out, regardless of costs, not so much for tactical reasons as for reasons of military prestige. As a MS history of the 2nd Division says:

Neither the enemy nor we could accept half possession of so important a position as Bouresches-Bois de Belleau. And the reasons for this were not merely tactical. A distinguished officer writing from the front...summed the matter up well by saying that the effect on both American and German morale and prestige, together with the necessity of securing the objective, made the occupation of the Bois de Belleau imperative; to this he might have

---

[190] 2nd Div Box 33, 54.3. 1st Corps memo of 26 Jun (2nd Div Box 35, 63.15) that defined the gas danger zone as the area NE of line Lizy sur Ourcq-la Ferte sous Jouarre-Sablonnieres, and the gas alert zone as the area NE of Villers-le Vasle-Martigny-Marigny-la Voie de Chatel-la Croisette, including villages and battery positions in Coupru and Domptin.

Even after the experience in June, gas discipline remained a problem. In mid-July, while the 2nd Div was in the Soissons sector, there was a report of "many instances of men going about without their respirators" both in the danger zone and in the alert zone. "In one instance a Major and his staff were found messing in a shelter without their respirators, the respirators being in another shelter about fifty feet distant; this battalion headquarters was but a short distance from the front lines and was in a good position for a gas bombardment." Rpt of Visit...July 18 to 23, by Lt H.W. Brown (AEF GHQ Box 1727, fol P, Item 9, G-5 Schools of the Line; cf. 2nd Div Box 85, 11.4, Hist of 2nd Eng, p. 3).

added that a grave crisis in French internal politics made it equally essential that no serious risk should be incurred, and yet that a success should be won.[191]

The Germans agreed on the prestige element, for on 8 June they said:

Should the Americans on our front gain the upper hand only temporarily, this may have the most unfavorable influence on the morale of the Entente and on the continuation of the war. In the fighting which now confronts us we are not concerned about the occupation or non-occupation of this or that unimportant woods or village but rather with the question as to whether Anglo-American propaganda, that the American Army is a match or even superior to the German, will be successful.[192]

How will the American troops conduct themselves in a major offensive? Therein lay the real significance of the combat for Belleau Wood.[193]

In this battle for prestige, the Germans were perpetually astonished by the willingness of the Americans to accept high casualties. They were also confronted with the task of explaining their loss of positions despite those casualties. Initially, much of their trouble was ascribed to the epidemic gas sickness among their troops, brought on in part by exhaustion and the French war gasses. Later, the tactical disposition and performance of Corps Conta itself shared the blame for their misfortunes. The commander of the 87th Division reported that on relieving the 28th Division he at once repaired the fatal error of that division, by organizing his forces in depth. But it was too late.

---

[191] The Second Division at Chateau Thierry (2nd Div Box 77).

[192] Daily Rpt, 28th Div Hq (Item 164, 1st Annex, War Diaries 2).

[193] Tr of monograph, Ernst Otto, The Fighting for Belleau Wood, p. 2 (2nd Div Box 31, 33.9).

From June 20 to 24 the Americans attacked the battalion located in the wood a total of 15 times with strong patrols, in strength up to two entire companies. Each time the attack collapsed in front of our lines with very heavy losses....The attacks initially took place entirely without preparation; next, supported by surprise rifle grenade fire, and then with gradually increasing artillery box barrage fire and, in the end, with the French participating....At 10:15 p.m. (on 25 June, the last day) only remnants of the five (German) participating companies were left.[194]

An operations report to the German Highest Command said: "An engagement in Belleau Wood is a typical example proving that the rigid unyielding holding of terrain, particularly in unfortified positions, always means a beginning accompanied by heaviest casualties and generally terminating in failure." These casualties resulted, the report went on, because the front line had been established as the main line of resistance and combat forces without fields of fire had been massed on the north edge of Belleau Wood.[195]

From the American point of view, the explanation of the operation was simple. The French order of 3 June, that the 2nd Division hold its positions before the advancing Germans "at all costs," had been obeyed. No record has been found while preparing this report that the order was ever questioned in any way. Not even the inability to retaliate in equal volume with HE or with gas seems ever to have been offered as a qualification of the operation. The French were skeptical of the fighting qualities of the inexperienced American troops. The 2nd Division, advancing in the attack in squad columns, was determined to prove its ability to take it. The two kilometers of terrain won

---

[194] Maj Gen Feldtkeller, Report Concerning the Combat in Belleau Wood, 29 Jun (Items 77-78, War Diaries 3).

[195] Opns Rpt, CofS Hq Army Group German Crown Prince, 8 Jul (Item 75, 87th Inf Div Rpts, War Diaries 3).

by the troops of the 2nd Division in those thirty-five days of combat were achieved in spite of the efforts, at one time and another, of elements of ten German divisions to keep them from it.

www.ingramcontent.com/pod-product-compliance
Lightning Source LLC
Chambersburg PA
CBHW050503110426
42742CB00018B/3353